Shimmy
Shimmy
Shimmy
Like My
Sister Kate

NIKKI
GIOVANNI

Shimmy Shimmy Shimmy Like My Sister Kate

Looking at the
Harlem Renaissance
Through Poems

HENRY HOLT
AND COMPANY
NEW YORK

Henry Holt and Company, Inc.
Publishers since 1866
115 West 18th Street
New York, New York 10011

Henry Holt is a registered
trademark of Henry Holt and Company, Inc.

Published in Canada by Fitzhenry & Whiteside Ltd.,
195 Allstate Parkway, Markham, Ontario L3R 4T8.

Library of Congress Cataloging-in-Publication Data
Shimmy shimmy shimmy like my sister Kate: looking at the Harlem Renaissance
through poems / edited by Nikki Giovanni.
    p.   cm.
Includes bibliographical references and index.
    Summary: Includes poems by such authors as Paul Laurence Dunbar, Langston
Hughes, Countee Cullen, Gwendolyn Brooks, and Amiri Baraka, with commentary
and a discussion of the development of African American arts known as the
Harlem Renaissance.
    1. Young adult poetry, American—Afro-American authors. 2. American poetry—
Afro-American authors—History and criticism. 3. American poetry—20th century—
History and criticism. 4. American poetry—20th century. 5. Afro-Americans in
literature. 6. Afro-Americans—Poetry. 7. Harlem Renaissance. [1. American poetry—
Afro-American authors—History and criticism. 2. American poetry—Afro-American
authors—Collections. 3. Afro-Americans—Poetry. 4. Harlem Renaissance.]
I. Giovanni, Nikki.
PS591.N4S55   1995   811'.50809283'08996073—dc20   95-38617

ISBN 0-8050-3494-3 / First Edition—1996
Printed in the United States of America on acid-free paper. ∞
10 9 8 7 6 5 4 3 2 1

An extension of this copyright page appears on pages 187–189.

I have been fortunate in my publishing career, which now is approaching a quarter century, to have had many very fine to excellent editors. All writers know our weaknesses as well as our strengths, and I am lucky to have had editors who have helped me be sure that whatever offensive thing I am saying I mean to say; whatever compliment I am paying I mean to pay. While I would never think of myself as difficult to work with, the news of January '95 threw not only this book but my life into a tizzy. My editor, Marc Aronson, sent flowers, good wishes, definite messages that if this book never was completed all he wanted was for my health to improve; he took time to help me clothes-shop when I was on my feet, took me to a great little restaurant in SoHo, and cheered me on in ways way beyond the call of duty. This book is a witness to the steadfastness of Marc . . . and I thank him.

⁓ CONTENTS

• *This symbol is used to indicate a stanza break within a poem wherever such breaks are lost in pagination.*

This is not a textbook, though it contains great African-American history. It is not lit crit, though we will look at some poems and some lines in great detail. It is a personal set of responses to this poetry informed by what I feel as much as what I think. There are stories I have been told that I want to share; there are attitudes I want to explore. Science teaches us matter is neither created nor destroyed. This can only mean that which was, is. All people study their history, whether self-consciously as "history," or as a series of stories, songs, ways of doing things, even what we cook and how we cook it. There is a story about that—about the young man who married a young woman. "The rice," he told her, "is the most important part of the meal." Wanting to please her husband, who was a good man and was kind, the wife learned very quickly to make excellent, fluffy rice. She did notice, however, that each time her husband sat down to dinner, he would salt his food. She, thinking she had not put enough salt in it, kept adding more salt each dinner. One evening, about a week or so later, the young husband could take it no longer. "My God, woman," he cried, "this food is briny!" Of course the husband, in my opinion, should never have shaken salt without first tasting the food, and the wife, had she been more relaxed, would have recognized that her husband was one of those people who like to shake salt, but since neither communicated, we came to briny food. Well, let me communicate. I think the world moves in cycles. The old spiritual tells us "every round gets higher, higher." I agree. I could have called this foray into the past "Give Me a Pig Foot and a Bottle of Beer," but somehow that didn't seem as classy as *Shimmy Shimmy Shimmy Like My Sister Kate.* And common sense tells us whereas we may go to a public dance and take a chance on strangers, we will not break bread other than with friends.

Shimmy Shimmy Shimmy Like My Sister Kate

Shimmy Shimmy Shimmy is an anthology that looks at the Harlem Renaissance through poems, though it includes poems that were written by modern authors as well as by people writing before the Harlem Renaissance. Why this range? The answer is in the name.

"Renaissance" is actually a very unusual term to use for the flowering of the arts in Harlem between 1917 and 1935. To say there is a *renaissance* is to say that there is a *re*birth or a *re*flowering, and there would be certainly those who would question, well, where was the original flowering? If you go back to 1619, with Africans landing in Virginia as slaves, and coming through that kind of wilderness, where would the flowering be? And yet if one would choose to be cosmic—I choose always to be cosmic—you would say that there was a divine intervention that wanted to put African people in America.

If we are going to be cosmic, we would have to say there were golden ages in Africa. If that was the case, then the Harlem Renaissance was connected to the great kingdoms of Songhay and Mali, and to the kingdoms of Egypt, but it would also be connected to the great kingdoms that came out of the Sudan, that came out of Zimbabwe—all of these great flowerings throughout history. So the Harlem Renaissance was the first American flowering of the black people.

I'm not a scholar. I'm not trying to approach this book on a scholarly basis. I don't want somebody calling me up and saying, "Well, good Lord, you can't possibly suggest a connection from ancient Africa to modern America." Yet in feeling there is a link. And I think connection is important, because if we recognize the African connection, then we can also see a kinship with the other renaissances—the Greek, and Roman, the Italian, even the British. So to see a link is not to exclude.

If we are looking at a renaissance, a rebirth, where do we begin? What fascinated me, as I tried to look at the poems that I have chosen to look at, is that every time we do slavery, every time we look at the institution of slavery, we always come up with a dry day. We come up with a sunny day. When you think about slaves, you think about the sun comes up and the slaves get up—and they clearly did not brush their teeth or bathe or put their deodorant on, or check their nails—but they got up and had to go into the fields. So I have always wondered, what do you do if you are a slave on a rainy day?

I have always been fascinated by a rainy day in Georgia, a rainy day in South Carolina. On a rainy day in South Carolina you probably did work, because in South Carolina you had the rice plantations. But a rainy day in, say, Mississippi is going to be a very heavy rain. To be historical we have to start with Virginia. If you say to yourself, Okay, what did the slaves do on a rainy day in Georgetown? Well, I like to think that they contemplated the universe. From that came songs, and sermons, and poetry.

We can go back to the slaves, and back even further to Africa. But I had to begin somewhere, and I chose Paul Laurence Dunbar. I wanted to start my experience of the Harlem Renaissance with freedom. I didn't pick the first free person—you have to draw a line somewhere. I think Phyllis Wheatley was a wonderful poet and a great woman. There is Jupiter Hammon and there could be a case built for Frederick Douglass being one of the premier people who helped to give birth, as it were, to the Harlem Renaissance. I chose Dunbar. He was—and this was a great achievement—a popular poet.

I know that people don't like popularity in the arts. I am

always amazed at how we disparage the fact that a poet can be heard. He was not only heard by white Americans, he was published in the magazines of his time. He was revered, but simple, clear. Paul Laurence Dunbar was directly connected to Langston Hughes, and Dunbar's poems are always being recited in churches, are always being recited at important meetings, important gatherings. His work creates a feeling of community. That is what I learned from him.

I think the written word is by nature political. In the second phase of his career, Langston Hughes, like Paul Dunbar, took his work to the people. He also said, Okay, I write poetry, yes, but I can also write a newspaper column; so he wrote a newspaper column. I can also write a novel; so he wrote a novel. I can also write an autobiography, and that's what he did. Anything, any way of getting by, is better than depending on some other human being to tell you whether or not you are any good. You may as well go out and please the people.

This need is what makes artists the quintessential capitalists: we are always having to please a lot of people. We didn't luck into something. This is not a natural resource that we are mining. This is something that we have to go out and do. To please a lot of people—it sounds a lot easier than it is—you have to have an honest product. You have to have something that's useful so that people who are on margins, poor people, are willing to support it.

I like it, though. I like the necessity to go to the people, and I like the necessity to please the people. We're not talking about reporters who write about the three-headed spaceman who came and impregnated my unborn dog. We are talking about putting out a product that describes the people, that describes and elicits the best of people who didn't have a voice, who didn't have a way of artistically defending themselves.

The art of the Harlem Renaissance was created for people who were the butt of jokes from everyone else in the country. It was like a huge funniness to be black. To be a black woman was to be fat and really rather witty, running the household and enjoying it so very much that you just never wanted to go home to your own family. It was just so much fun being in the kitchen while Miss Ann was out playing bridge, and the master comes home and you could tell him, "Oh, honey, Mr. Smith, you better not have any more coffee," or "Mr. John, you better not drink any more." You were tired of it. Black people were tired of being portrayed. They were sick of mammies and *Birth of a Nation*. It was only artists like Countee Cullen, like James Weldon Johnson—it was only these artists who were trying to say, "We are people of dignity and strength."

The Renaissance came in the arts, but it was the result of new social conditions. In the early twentieth century blacks came up north in great numbers. In 1890, only one out of every seventy persons in Manhattan was black. By 1930, it was one in nine. Blacks came north to work in the war industries and to escape from lynching. This great migration created a huge need for housing. Harlem was a white neighborhood, but a smart black real-estate agent thought to himself, "I'll rent these apartments to black people because they'll pay more." He was right, because blacks had so little housing that they would pay more for the same things.

In Harlem, then, black business and black professions flourished along with the arts. You had pharmacists, you had dentists, you had doctors. This, too, was part of the flowering. You had Harlem Hospital, which was a great teaching hospital. There were schoolteachers in the Renaissance, and Alain Locke, the first black Rhodes scholar, played a big part in it. This was a flowering of business, of ideas, and of spirit.

I called this book *Shimmy Shimmy Shimmy Like My Sister Kate* because ordinary people, black people—if they didn't do anything else—ordinary people took up the new spirit in terms of creating themselves through dance.

When we get to the Renaissance, to the 1920s, we are, as my grandmother would say, we're feeling our Cheerios. She used to laugh about that all the time. People were free to express themselves. The shimmy wasn't just the dance, it wasn't "Shimmy, Shimmy," it was the freedom of your own body. You owned it and you could celebrate it. You could rejoice with it. So dance was one of the arts, and actually if black people were not artificially restricted, we would have excelled in all forms. Clearly blacks took over modern dance. If we were not segregated, there would just be no American ballet without premier dancers being black. But you know, "Black women's butts are too big," and "Black women's breasts are too fat." What it is is their skin is too dark. We had the same problem in opera; but almost anything that blacks are free to compete in in the arts we have taken on, and we have triumphed.

One of the most important arts of the Renaissance period was theater. In the nineteenth century minstrelsy was popular—that was whites in blackface taking off on what they saw blacks doing to entertain themselves. As the minstrel show evolved it turned into vaudeville. But by the twenties there were all-black shows on Broadway. The most famous was *Blackbirds of 1928*. Then some avant-garde playwrights started to use black actors, like Paul Robeson, in white plays. And soon white people were coming up to Harlem. It was still a segregated society, but not like today.

There was this window, approximately between World War I and World War II, when whites still came uptown. They took the subway, the A train. When you think about New York subways, you think of blacks and Puerto Ricans, and you think of knives and guns, and, oh my goodness, a white person shouldn't get on a subway because he'll get killed. But in the old days subways were like buses or trolleys or anything else. They were respectable. You'd wear your tux and tails, and you took the A train and got off at 125th Street, and from there you took a cab. And you went to dance and to listen to jazz.

If there is any one thing that is totally undisputed, totally undisputed, it is that black Americans created the music of America. That goes back to the spirituals and ahead to today. In Harlem you could hear Duke Ellington, Fats Waller, W. C. Handy, Louis Armstrong, and many others. They were the sound of the Renaissance. But its voice came from outside of the arts, it came from three great men. One of them had already died, one lived throughout most of the century, and one was right there in the center of it. They are Booker T. Washington, W. E. B. Du Bois, and Marcus Garvey.

I've always liked Booker T., because I know what Booker T. did was not easy. Booker was a West Virginian who actually walked, and this is a pretty big state, who actually walked over to Hampton, got there, didn't have any money or anything else but was willing to work, and they let him stay because he worked hard, like most people who are self-made. He thought that honest, hard work will surely out, and in some cases—the luck of the draw being what it is—honest, hard work will out.

What he wanted to do was start a school. Again this had to be a huge joke, a black school in the middle of redneck Alabama. Tuskegee is still a good hour's drive from Atlanta as the crow flies on the expressway. Tuskegee, you are talking *redneck,* red dirt, dangerous situation. It took a special kind of guy just to end up not being lynched. They gave him this land because it wasn't any good for anything else. Nobody thought in any way, shape, or form would he succeed. It is very hard to get people to believe in your dreams, but Booker T. did.

Washington was able to convince ordinary people, ordinary workmen, not even craftsmen, just ordinary workmen, that they should build the bricks for his school. But these were not ordinary bricks. There are two ways to make bricks. Bricks that are going to be outside have to be fired, baked. But how do you fire the bricks? How do you make the oven to fire the bricks? You make do with what you have: you use sun-baked bricks to make the oven. You are going to get only so many bricks out of it before your sun-baked bricks break down, but you hope you'll get enough bricks so that when the sun-baked bricks break down, you have the fired bricks, and then you use them.

Washington was amazing because he could convince people to make the sun-baked bricks, to fire the bricks, and to build his school building. Anybody will help you build a building if you dig a hole or lay it out. Then anybody can say, "I can see where the building is going." But if you are standing there telling somebody, "We are going to bake these bricks in the sun and then from that we are going to make a real oven," nobody is going to do that. He was a very persuasive man. Once he got one building built, then he could use that to build another, and he did.

Washington did something else that was quite brilliant. He went over to Iowa because he'd heard about George Washington Carver, and he knew he needed a scientist. He knew that as much as anything he needed a scientist, and he went over to Iowa and he convinced Dr. Carver that he had a laboratory, which was a joke because Carver gets there and there is not even a beaker there. It's like, here it is, it's upstairs, and Carver is thinking, "Oh, my God, I agreed to come here and he says this is what we've got, this ground, and you can plant peanuts." And Carver went on to do a lot with those peanuts. You have to give Booker T. Washington credit—people try to put him down—for recognizing and going after genius, which is what he did.

What Washington was trying to say was, for people who don't have anything, we have to make sure they get something. And that's what Tuskegee has stood for, and in fact that's what Tuskegee still stands for.

One of the men that took a real potshot at him was W. E. B. Du Bois. By any standard Du Bois was a genius. I don't think anybody has ever said that he wasn't an extremely bright guy. He graduated from high school. He had to stay out of school for a year and then got some scholarships and then he went to Fisk.

He finished at Fisk in 1888 and went on to obtain a second bachelor's degree from Harvard, graduating cum laude two years later. Then he went to study for his Ph.D. in history at the University of Berlin. In the end he was the first black American to earn a doctorate at Harvard. This was a very bright guy.

If William Edward Burghardt Du Bois could have single-handedly pulled black Americans up from slavery and into the citizenship of their fellow Americans, there is no doubt that he would have done so. He had this great intellect, what Hercule Poirot would have called "the little gray cells," that he put at the disposal of his race. But he also had, I think it fair to say, this great impatience with those who were less capable than he. I have a Du Bois problem not because Du Bois wasn't a good man, but because he wanted so much more for the people than they could possibly want for themselves that he became disenchanted with America and disappointed with black people. Du Bois, in his great work *The Souls of Black Folk,* experienced the same duality that he described: "One ever feels his twoness—an American, a Negro . . . two souls, two thoughts, two unreconciled stirrings; two warring ideals in one dark body whose dogged strength alone keeps it from being torn asunder." This was very profound, this thought, and it remains with us today as much as Du Bois pointing out: "The problem of the twentieth century is the problem of the color line." Perhaps to keep some of the hurt away, perhaps to prove, much as Martin Luther King, Jr., tried to prove, that not all black men were laughing, joking goof-offs, he made it a point of personal pride not to smile while in graduate school. Du Bois set out to be a detached scholar. His was pioneering work in sociology, in looking at a people—and had he not been of color, he would be considered the father of sociology today. *The Souls of Black Folk* was a slim volume that sets forth Du Bois's hopes and dreams for his people. It first appeared in 1903; it remains in print today.

Booker T. Washington, in his famous Atlanta Exposition

speech of 1895, had said that blacks should be willing to give up the right to vote in exchange for increased opportunities in business and agriculture, as well as protection from rednecks. Du Bois thought that this was terrible, and that Washington was giving away what he called "the manhood rights of voting." I don't have a problem with that, but I do have a problem with Du Bois squaring off as if Booker T. Washington were a traitor to his race. By the twenties this was a big split in the community. There was Booker T.—or his followers; he had died in 1915— and we had W. E. B., and how do we negotiate this space?

Well, a man from Jamaica had heard about Booker T. Washington. He'd heard about his school in Tuskegee and he thought, "I should learn what this man has learned so I can help my people." Marcus Garvey had gone over to the Panama Canal. He was a newspaper reporter looking at the canal, because more Jamaicans died digging the Panama Canal than anybody else. Garvey thought, "My people should know about this," so he started trying to get passage to America. When he finally got the money to come to America, unfortunately Dr. Washington was dead.

Garvey was in New York, and there was no point to go to Alabama because there was nobody in Alabama that he thought he should see, so he stayed there. He said to himself, "What is it that we need?" He thought, "We need a group." So Garvey started the United Negro Improvement Association.

Everybody thought he was funny at first because he wore feathered hats, and he had his parades. But what he had was the biggest movement ever of black people in the United States. Marcus had the expression "Africa for Africans at home and abroad." That is a very inflammatory kind of speech, because it's the reverse of segregation.

Everybody thinks it's a great idea to keep the black people down. Even Lincoln would have preferred to send blacks to Africa, but it was too expensive. Yet when a black man came up—and this was again the first time that they had to hear it—when a black man comes up and says, "Africa for Africans at home and abroad," implying "We don't want to live with you," then everybody is upset. Suddenly whites were hurt: "Oh, you don't like us?" This is some kind of impossible joke.

The Garvey movement was wonderful. It gave people a sense of power. It empowered your nurses and your street sweepers. Ordinary laborers were empowered in a way that previously came only to deacons in the church. Garvey was trying to show black Americans that we are a great people. We have fallen clearly upon hard times, but it is not unusual in life cycles to do so, and it is now time to lift ourselves up.

The federal government hated Garvey. They hated him because he was a good organizer. They hated him because he had a great movement, and of course they trumped up some charges of mail fraud to deport him. Whether they were alive or dead, in America or overseas, Washington, Du Bois, and Garvey all helped shape the Renaissance. It was the writers who made it happen.

The writers brought the message. They said we are militant; we are strong; we are black; we are proud, and we are going to fight a war with words. If I would be granted anything, I would say to black Americans: we are the ones who perfected the "war of words."

Throughout their history in America, black people have had this choice: we can either fight the war for freedom physically, or we can fight the war with words. Physically we would have lost. That was very clear. Somebody could say, "How do you know, you didn't really try." If the Vietnamese had looked at the statistics they would probably figure they couldn't beat France or America, except they had home-court advantage. It is always very helpful if you are going to fight a war with a bigger power to fight it in a terrain that they don't understand. That's how the Vietnamese did win their war. But here in America, we were going to have a fight of propaganda, and everybody wanted the writers to be on board.

The only problem with fighting with words is that it makes it hard to laugh. Nobody liked to laugh; they didn't want to laugh at any part of black life, and they didn't feel that people should. They wanted only to have uplifting ideas that blacks and white would see and say, "Aren't we wonderful people." But I think you have to show everything in order for a people to be free.

You have to be able to show those things that some of us think are good, and those things that some of us would think are bad. If some people had had their way, we would have suppressed jazz. We would never have allowed "Shimmy, Shimmy, Shimmy." We would never have allowed the rent parties. We would never have allowed a Bessie Smith to sing "Give Me a Pig Foot and a Bottle of Beer." We would never have allowed a song like "My Handyman," which is a really bawdy song. We would have suppressed all of that in a desire to put forth this Puritan image that black people are really wonderful and deserving of freedom. Freedom isn't something you deserve.

The Harlem Renaissance showed that you can't earn freedom, you have to assume it. You have to take it. We had people in the sixties who also thought they should tell black people what to say. They said that artists should speak for the militant needs of the people. I like militance. The problem is that in order to be free you have to use all of your expression. You have to make use of everything, whether some people consider it good or some people consider it bad.

The Harlem Renaissance is the pivotal period that shows—as a people—these are the possibilities; these are the probabilities; these are things that we may achieve and these are things we probably won't, but we hope for a better world and we support one another in whatever desires we have to move forward.

Sure, there were people in Harlem, and there were people in black America, who didn't even know that there was a Renaissance going on. Later on, there were people that didn't know there was a civil rights movement. Some of them found out when they got shot. Some of them found out when they got bombed. Some of them found out when they were trying to go to the bathroom and something else happened, and some of them found out when they just felt that there was something in the air that felt different. When you are part of great movements, when you are alive during them, you feel it.

I can't help but think that whoever was around when Michelangelo was painting, or Leonardo da Vinci, knew that something was in the air. When Dante wrote *The Divine Comedy,* there were many people who couldn't read Italian. The people in whose language he wrote it were essentially illiterate, but they knew something had happened. Same with the Harlem Renaissance: everybody knew something had happened. They may not have been able to always tell you what, and it probably was annoying that there were so many places right there in Harlem where black patrons were not welcome. But they knew.

The Renaissance was a great flowering. It was a people deciding that we will wage war with images. We will wage war with creativity, with words, with our souls. We will not stoop to be what you think we are, nor will we stoop to be what you are trying to make us. We are going, in the words of the old spiritual, "to plant our feet on higher ground." That's what is outstanding about this period, and I think that's why I wanted to link from the beginning, from the back all the way up front, because it's still affecting us.

This is not so long ago. We were talking about Gwen Brooks and Margaret Walker, for example. Langston could be alive if he hadn't had the bad luck of going to a bad hospital and contracting a disease while he was there, but when you start to look at it, there are people who are still alive from that period. There are no more Garveyites, but Garvey was a major influence on Elijah Muhammad, and the Nation of Islam still exists. There are Malcolmites, and Malcolm was an offshoot of the Nation of Islam, so it is all there. We are all the children of a Countee Cullen. Really my generation is the grandchild of Langston simply because we, too, wanted to take our art out to the people.

I'm not a young writer anymore, and yet there are links. There is a line, and if this life was a mountain we'd all be climbing it. A mountain-climbing team is only as good as the person in front of you or the person behind. It's a chain. It's a little better if the person behind you has a problem; you can disconnect from him a lot easier than if the person in front of you has a problem. Then you really are going to fall, you know that, and you are going to die on that mountain. I wanted to look at the people in front of us, and I know that's a very secure footing we have. In this book, I wanted to share that with everyone coming up the mountain.

⟶ W. E. B. Du Bois (1868–1963)

The Song of the Smoke

I am the smoke king,
I am black.
I am swinging in the sky.
I am ringing worlds on high:
I am the thought of the throbbing mills,
I am the soul toil kills,
I am the ripple of trading rills,

Up I'm curling from the sod,
I am whirling home to God.
I am the smoke king,
I am black.

I am the smoke king,
I am black.
I am wreathing broken hearts,
I am sheathing devils' darts;
Dark inspiration of iron times,
Wedding the toil of toiling climes
Shedding the blood of bloodless crimes.

Down I lower in the blue,
Up I tower toward the true,
I am the smoke king,
I am black.

I am the smoke king,
I am black.

I am darkening with song,
I am hearkening to wrong;
I will be black as blackness can,
The blacker the mantle the mightier the man,
My purpl'ing midnights no day dawn may ban.

I am carving God in night,
I am painting hell in white.
I am the smoke king,
I am black.

I am the smoke king,
I am black.

I am cursing ruddy morn,
I am nursing hearts unborn;
Souls unto me are as mists in the night,
I whiten my blackmen, I beckon my white,
What's the hue of a hide to a man in his might!

Sweet Christ, pity toiling lands!
Hail to the smoke king,
Hail to the black!

It is interesting that a guy like W. E. B. Du Bois, who actually did very little, I should imagine, with his hands, wrote about "I am the smoke king." Without the labor, both free and slave, of African Americans this country would still be a wilderness.

Du Bois wrote poetry. He also wrote novels, and he is most famous for his sociological study *The Souls of Black Folk*. The surprising thing is that he used his poetry to celebrate black labor, and not from a distance. Du Bois was always known for keeping his emotional distance. But here he takes on the voice of the black worker as his own: "I am carving God in night, / I am painting hell in white. / I am the smoke king."

This is a very strong statement about how he views the world. He will find more intellectual ways of dealing with black life as he moves on, but this is direct:

> *I am cursing ruddy morn,*
> *I am nursing hearts unborn;*
> *Souls unto me are as mists in the night,*
> *I whiten my blackmen, I beckon my white,*
> *What's the hue of a hide to a man in his might!*

This is fascinating, Du Bois the superintellectual as the voice of the labor and energy of black Americans. Hail to the smoke king, Hail to the black!

The Creation

A Negro Sermon

And God stepped out on space,
And He looked around and said,
"I'm lonely—
I'll make me a world."

And far as the eye of God could see
Darkness covered everything,
Blacker than a hundred midnights
Down in a cypress swamp.

Then God smiled,
And the light broke,
And the darkness rolled up on one side,
And the light stood shining on the other,
And God said, *"That's good!"*

Then God reached out and took the light in His hands,
And God rolled the light around in His hands,
Until He made the sun;
And He set that sun a-blazing in the heavens.
And the light that was left from making the sun
God gathered up in a shining ball
And flung across the darkness,
Spangling the night with the moon and stars.

Then down between
The darkness and the light
He hurled the world;
And God said, *"That's good!"*

Then God himself stepped down—
And the sun was on His right hand,
And the moon was on His left;
The stars were clustered about His head,
And the earth was under His feet.
And God walked, and where He trod
His footsteps hollowed the valleys out
And bulged the mountains up.

Then He stopped and looked and saw
That the earth was hot and barren.
So God stepped out over to the edge of the world
And He spat out the seven seas;
He batted His eyes, and the lightnings flashed;
He clapped His hands, and the thunders rolled;
And the waters above the earth came down,
The cooling waters came down.

Then the green grass sprouted,
And the little red flowers blossomed,
The pine-tree pointed his finger to the sky,
And the oak spread out his arms;
The lakes cuddled down in the hollows of the ground,
And the rivers ran down to the sea;
And God smiled again,
And the rainbow appeared,
And curled itself around His shoulder.

Then God raised His arm and He waved His hand
Over the sea and over the land,
And He said, *"Bring forth! Bring forth!"*
And quicker than God could drop His hand,
Fishes and fowls
And beasts and birds
Swam the rivers and the seas,
Roamed the forests and the woods,
And split the air with their wings,
And God said, *"That's good!"*

Then God walked around
And God looked around
On all that He had made.
He looked at His sun,
And He looked at His moon,
And He looked at His little stars;
He looked on His world
With all its living things,
And God said, *"I'm lonely still."*

Then God sat down
On the side of a hill where He could think;
By a deep, wide river He sat down;
With His head in His hands,
God thought and thought,
Till He thought, *"I'll make me a man!"*

Up from the bed of the river
God scooped the clay;
And by the bank of the river
He kneeled Him down;
And there the great God Almighty,
Who lit the sun and fixed it in the sky,
Who flung the stars to the most far corner of the night,
Who rounded the earth in the middle of His hand—
This Great God,
Like a mammy bending over her baby,
Kneeled down in the dust
Toiling over a lump of clay
Till He shaped it in His own image;

Then into it He blew the breath of life,
And man became a living soul.
Amen. Amen.

The *Creation* is from James Weldon Johnson's collection of sermons entitled *God's Trombones*. Johnson went around and actually did what Zora Neale Hurston would do later, went around
and collected sermons and wrote them down. He had a dilemma
as to whether to put them into standard English or to put them
in dialect, in patois. He decided that he would write them out in
poetry so they would not read as a takeoff. Dunbar had given
some of the writers a problem because he wrote in that plantation patois which some people could take as if it were laughing
at black people, and Johnson wanted to show respect.

Normally when one hears *The Creation*, and I've been hearing
The Creation all my life, you hear: "And God stepped out on
space, / And He looked around and said, / *'I'm lonely*— / *I'll*

make me a world.'" It is read almost as an elocution contest. Everybody speaks from the diaphragm and speaks well. But about twenty or twenty-five years ago, I heard my friend and sister artist Val Ward, who is the founder of the Kuumba Theater in Chicago, I heard Val recite *The Creation* as a Baptist minister would speak it.

Val is from Mount Bayou, Mississippi. When she contemplated how this sermon would have been recited as it got passed from preacher to preacher, she realized it would have been recited in the traditional holiness sense, in the sense of the holy rollers, not in the sense of the Presbyterians but in the sense of the fundamentalist Baptists: "And *God* stepped out on space, huh," with that rhythm. That is impossible to put on a piece of paper, but it's that breath that they take, that step that they take.

You can see how, with that power, this would be a very entertaining sermon. You can see how people would actually be able to say, "Reverend Smith is coming to town and he will recite *The Creation,*" and people would come because they had heard about it or had even heard it before. It is certainly worthy of being heard again and again and again. I've been hearing it all my life, and I still enjoy hearing it very much.

It's also an important poem. I have no doubt as to why this sermon survived, because it is such an affirmation of life. It places black Americans squarely in the hands of the Lord. We have this God, like a mammy, sitting down by a mighty river and making man in his image. I would probably quarrel with what he made in his image. I still have to think he made woman as his partner. Nonetheless, he made human beings out of this dirt, this black soil at this mighty river, and I think it had to be just one of the great affirmations that black Americans, too, are in the bosom of God, that God created us and cares about us.

Johnson started to collect sermons because he had a sense of history, and he knew that if we didn't record these words they'd be lost. He was absolutely right. I remember John Killens always told a story about this. There was a little boy, and his father was telling him a story about the tigers and the lions. And the kid said, "Daddy, how come the tigers and the lions always lose? How come they always get defeated in the end, or beaten up in the end?" And his father said, "Well, son, that will always happen until the tigers and the lions learn how to write." That makes a lot of sense to me. In order to have a happy ending, in order to be triumphant, in order to be heroic, you have to tell your own story. The women's movement knows that; black people know that; brown people know that; yellow people know that. You have to be able to tell your own story in order to show that you are worthy—that you belong.

⟢ Paul Laurence Dunbar (1872–1906)

Paul Laurence Dunbar is just such an important figure because he was popular. I think that Dunbar, for lack of better words, "done good." In looking at his people he found us objects of his affection. He liked black people. Dunbar was a short, small, dark-skinned man, and I think he delighted in us.

I think of him as a liberator, as a Du Bois, or as a Booker T. Washington. He tried to build something. His gift was words. In trying to utilize it, he wanted to find the words of his people. Now, clearly, people use your art whatever way they want to use your art. You can only produce the art. To some people you sew some cloth together and you make a quilt. To other people you make a pattern for a dress. It is all just cloth you are sewing together. You make the cloth and somebody decides how it is used.

When Dunbar wrote his plantation ditties, I think he did it to try to maintain something of the speech of the people. In the same way, we in the sixties used what was called "street language"—double negatives, or what could be considered simply a more natural way of talking. I don't think that that was a put-down either. Probably in the year 3000 somebody is going to look back and see the kind of language that we used and say, "That's really ridiculous. Those people didn't like black people." Nothing could be farther from the truth.

We Wear the Mask

We wear the mask that grins and lies,
It hides our cheeks and shades our eyes,—
This debt we pay to human guile;
With torn and bleeding hearts we smile,
And mouth with myriad subtleties.

Why should the world be overwise,
In counting all our tears and sighs?
Nay, let them only see us, while
    We wear the mask.

We smile, but, O great Christ, our cries
To Thee from tortured souls arise.
We sing, but oh, the clay is vile
Beneath our feet, and long the mile;
But let the world dream otherwise,
    We wear the mask.

We Wear the Mask is so important because everybody does have a mask. There is no question that we all somehow or other protect ourselves. In Africa they make masks for ceremonies, and there are masks here in celebrations like Mardi Gras. A mask is used to hide—or to express—your other personality.

Dunbar is saying simply that there has been great pain in the lives of black people and we are trying not to have our wounds always be open. We recognize that behind these eyes is great pain, that we know what is happening to us. We are not stupid, forgetful people. We know what we have been through; we know exactly the price we've paid. We are talking about a people who recognize the tenuousness of both life and liberty, and of course we try to protect ourselves. We try to do something to keep people from continually hurting us.

Sympathy

I know what the caged bird feels, alas!
When the sun is bright on the upland slopes;
When the wind stirs soft through the springing grass,
And the river flows like a stream of glass;
When the first bird sings and the first bud opes,
And the faint perfume from its chalice steals—
I know what the caged bird feels!

I know why the caged bird beats his wing
Till its blood is red on the cruel bars;
For he must fly back to his perch and cling
When he fain would be on the bough a-swing;
And a pain still throbs in the old, old scars
And they pulse again with a keener sting—
I know why he beats his wing!

I know why the caged bird sings, ah me,
When his wing is bruised and his bosom sore,—
When he beats his bars and he would be free;
It is not a carol of joy or glee,
But a prayer that he sends from his heart's deep core,
But a plea, that upward to Heaven he flings—
I know why the caged bird sings!

Sympathy has one of the great lines in poetry. "I know what the caged bird feels!" To be a black American is to be proscribed. People want to control where you can go, what you can do, what your aspirations should be, and everybody has some use for you and everybody wants you to be useful for them but never for yourself, and it is not right.

Then Dunbar ended with his second great line: "I know why the caged bird sings!" That line has been used a million times. It comes right from Dunbar's poem, and he is right. We all know why. We understand what it feels, what it would hope for, and why it sings despite it all. It could beat its wings bloody, but it could also say, "Since this is where I am, I must find a way to make something wonderful happen."

Flying is an old metaphor. "I'm Going to Fly Away One of These Days" is an old gospel song. Dunbar is saying that the bird beats his wings against the bar until they are bloody and even at that he finds a way to sing, but everybody does whatever he can to be free.

We all would like to just lift ourselves and fly away, free as a bird, to our mountains. There are so many slave stories. Toni Morrison, of course, recounts slave stories in *Song of Solomon* where Solomon flew away. People just decided that they were going to leave. But we can take leave now, not just of our senses.

The song this bird is singing is "not a carol of joy or glee, / But a prayer," and all of life is a prayer. That's the one thing I would agree totally with. Life is a prayer. That's the only way it makes sense.

Look at the slaves. Dunbar is from Dayton, which puts him on the beginning of the northern end of the Underground Railroad. Clearly everybody is going to do what they can to be free: to find a way to lift their voices or to find a way to lift their bodies and lift their spirits. One of the things that slaves did, and I guess we'll keep saying that until people get tired of hearing it, but one of the things that slaves did that is so outstanding is that they found a way to lift their voices in the spirituals. They found a way to get their stories told and to put them in language that could be remembered, because they couldn't be written down. It is not going to get to books, it is going to have to come from an oral tradition. We know from our own Christian Bible that you can carry something four hundred, five hundred years before you write it down. We know from *The Iliad* and *The Odyssey* and things of that nature, *Song of Roland,* that people remember things. And of course in modern testament, the American slaves, black Americans, also passed their history along, despite everything else.

Like the slaves, Dunbar's bird is not singing because it is free. It is singing to relieve the tension. We want to abuse people, but we don't want them to take exception to that. We want them to understand why it is necessary. It is like Germans and Jews. "Well, we didn't really mean it. Sure, a couple of million people or so were killed, maybe five or six million, but gee, golly, you can understand how these things get out of hand. Why be bitter?" And we do the same thing to black Americans. We do the same thing to Native Americans. "Well, gee, how come you people are bitter?"

Of course people are bitter. Some of the spirituals are what Du Bois called "sorrow songs." "I've been 'buked and I've been scorned. I've been talked about sure as I'm born." I don't think of them as sorrow songs. I know that even when there is a you that is being compelled, there is another you that says, "This is not a part of me. I am somewhere else." That's flying, too.

A Negro Love Song

Seen my lady home las' night,
    Jump back, honey, jump back.
Hel' huh han' an' sque'z it tight,
    Jump back, honey, jump back.
Hyeahd huh sigh a little sigh,
Seen a light gleam f'om huh eye,
An' a smile go flittin' by—
    Jump back, honey, jump back.

Hyeahd de win' blow thoo de pine,
    Jump back, honey, jump back.
Mockin'-bird was singin' fine,
    Jump back, honey, jump back.
An' my hea't was beatin' so,
When I reached my lady's do',
Dat I couldn't ba' to go—
    Jump back, honey, jump back.

Put my ahm aroun' huh wais',
    Jump back, honey, jump back.
Raised huh lips an' took a tase,
    Jump back, honey, jump back.
Love me, honey, love me true?
Love me well ez I love you?
An' she answe'd, " 'Cose I do"—
    Jump back, honey, jump back.

I like *A Negro Love Song* for the same reason. It says that no matter what you do to me, I still am. I still exist. There is a part of me that, no matter what you do, I am not going to let you touch it. I'm going to fall in love. I have feelings and this is the way I express them. I am not going to act like all I do is court my lady in a way that white people never do. If you read books, when I was growing up even, you never thought white people had sex outside of marriage. And then I got older and started reading other books and I thought, "Oh, they're just like everybody else."

Dunbar writes, "Seen my lady home las' night." This is just a wonderful, joyful expression: Yeah, we have a lot of problems; nobody is saying we don't; nobody is saying we are overlooking them; nobody is saying we are forgetting them. But in the meantime, I did see my lady love last night. And I think that is really sweet because she loves him, too. So it is not going to be probably a happy ending. They get married, he is probably going to hit her. We can go through all of the trouble, but for this moment it is a love story. It's a love poem. It is a Negro love song, and I like that.

✍ Claude McKay (1890–1948)

If We Must Die

If we must die, let it not be like hogs
Hunted and penned in an inglorious spot,
While round us bark the mad and hungry dogs,
Making their mock at our accursed lot.
If we must die, O let us nobly die,
So that our precious blood may not be shed
In vain; then even the monsters we defy
Shall be constrained to honor us though dead!
O kinsmen! we must meet the common foe!
Though far outnumbered let us show us brave,
And for their thousand blows deal one deathblow!
What though before us lies the open grave?
Like men we'll face the murderous, cowardly pack,
Pressed to the wall, dying, but fighting back!

Claude McKay is going to be another color of a different horse,
as the old folks used to say. McKay was Jamaican, and he came
from a maroon background. Maroons were the slaves that es-
caped from the plantations and went up into the mountains.
They have had their revenge upon the world because the best
coffee on the entire planet Earth is Jamaican Blue Mountain and
they charge thirty dollars for a half a pound of it. You can't even
buy it by the pound; nobody sells it at sixty dollars a pound.

The maroons ran up to the hills of Jamaica. The hills of Jamaica are something to see because the maroons are the people

who bring us jerk pork. They would cook their pigs, wild boars actually, over an open fire. They would put them on a spit. The English would be down in Kingston, down in the city, down in the lowlands that made up the plantations. They could look up—and you could, too, if we were in Jamaica right now—they looked up into the hills and saw the smoke.

For those of us who are Appalachian, it is sort of like watching the clouds come off the Smoky Mountains. You can begin to see exactly why the Smoky Mountains are called the Smoky Mountains, because you can look up and see the smoke. The maroons could do that, and in the old days the English had to march up; they couldn't even take mules or anything. They had to walk up. By the time they walked from where they were to where the maroons were cooking, the maroons had eaten and had moved on.

Claude McKay comes, in other words, from a fighting people. He is not going to give in. He is not saying we should die—but he is saying, if we must, let us not die like cowards. "Let us show us brave."

People didn't care for McKay saying things like that because, again, when we abuse people, we don't want them to be upset about it; and we certainly didn't want to hear people saying blacks should fight back because, my goodness, if blacks start fighting back, somebody is going to get hurt. But of course somebody needed to be hurt. All Claude was saying is, "This isn't right what's happening, and we should demand redress." It is a powerful point.

Dark Symphony

1
Allegro Moderato

Black Crispus Attucks taught
        Us how to die
Before white Patrick Henry's bugle breath
Uttered the vertical
        Transmitting cry:
"Yea, give me liberty or give me death."

Waifs of the auction block,
        Men black and strong
The juggernauts of despotism withstood,
Loin-girt with faith that worms
        Equate the wrong
And dust is purged to create brotherhood.

No Banquo's ghost can rise
        Against us now,
Aver we hobnailed Man beneath the brute,
Squeezed down the thorns of greed
        On Labor's brow,
Garroted lands and carted off the loot.

2
Lento Grave

The centuries-old pathos in our voices
Saddens the great white world,
And the wizardry of our dusky rhythms
Conjures up shadow-shapes of ante-bellum years:

Black slaves singing *One More River to Cross*
In the torture tombs of slave-ships,
Black slaves singing *Steal Away to Jesus*
In jungle swamps,
Black slaves singing *The Crucifixion*
In slave-pens at midnight,
Black slaves singing *Swing Low, Sweet Chariot*
In cabins of death,
Black slaves singing *Go Down, Moses*
In the canebrakes of the Southern Pharaohs.

3
Andante Sostenuto

They tell us to forget
The Golgotha we tread . . .
We who are scourged with hate,
A price upon our head.
They who have shackled us
Require of us a song,
They who have wasted us
Bid us condone the wrong.

                                                        .

They tell us to forget
Democracy is spurned.
They tell us to forget
The Bill of Rights is burned.
Three hundred years we slaved,
We slave and suffer yet:
Though flesh and bone rebel,
They tell us to forget!

Oh, how can we forget
Our human rights denied?
Oh, how can we forget
Our manhood crucified?
When Justice is profaned
And plea with curse is met,
When Freedom's gates are barred,
Oh, how can we forget?

4

Tempo Primo

The New Negro strides upon the continent
In seven-league boots . . .
The New Negro
Who sprang from the vigor-stout loins
Of Nat Turner, gallows-martyr for Freedom,
Of Joseph Cinquez, Black Moses of the Amistad Mutiny,
Of Frederick Douglass, oracle of the Catholic Man,
Of Sojourner Truth, eye and ear of Lincoln's legions,
Of Harriet Tubman, Saint Bernard of the Underground
    Railroad.   •

The New Negro
Breaks the icons of his detractors,
Wipes out the conspiracy of silence,
Speaks to *his* America:

"My history-moulding ancestors
Planted the first crops of wheat on these shores,
Built ships to conquer the seven seas,
Erected the Cotton Empire,
Flung railroads across a hemisphere,
Disemboweled the earth's iron and coal,
Tunneled the mountains and bridged rivers,
Harvested the grain and hewed forests,
Sentineled the Thirteen Colonies,
Unfurled Old Glory at the North Pole,
Fought a hundred battles for the Republic."

The New Negro:
His giant hands fling murals upon high chambers,
His drama teaches a world to laugh and weep,
His music leads continents captive,
His voice thunders the Brotherhood of Labor,
His science creates seven wonders,
His Republic of Letters challenges the Negro-baiters.

The New Negro,
Hard-muscled, Fascist-hating, Democracy-ensouled,
Strides in seven-league boots
Along the Highway of Today
Toward the Promised Land of Tomorrow!

5
Larghetto

None in the Land can say
To us black men Today:
You send the tractors on their bloody path,
And create Okies for *The Grapes of Wrath.*
You breed the slum that breeds a *Native Son*
To damn the good earth Pilgrim Fathers won.

None in the Land can say
To us black men Today:
You dupe the poor with rags-to-riches tales,
And leave the workers empty dinner pails.
You stuff the ballot box, and honest men
Are muzzled by your demagogic din.

None on the Land can say
To us black men Today·
You smash stock markets with your coined blitzkriegs,
And make a hundred million guinea pigs.
You counterfeit our Christianity,
And bring contempt upon Democracy.

None in the Land can say
To us black men Today:
You prowl when citizens are fast asleep,
And hatch Fifth Column plots to blast the deep
Foundations of the State and leave the Land
A vast Sahara with a Fascist brand.

6
Tempo di Marcia

Out of abysses of Illiteracy,
Through labyrinths of Lies,
Across waste lands of Disease . . .
We advance!

Out of dead-ends of Poverty,
Through wildernesses of Superstition,
Across barricades of Jim Crowism . . .
We advance!

With the Peoples of the World . . .
We advance!

One of the advantages of being a student at Fisk University in the middle sixties was that John Oliver Killens was invited down to be the writer in residence, and John started having an annual Black Arts Festival which was very nice. When he held the first Black Arts Festival, he invited Melvin Tolson to come.

Melvin was really a bright man. It was such a treasure because he was a tall, thin man and very, very energetic, and who would have thought Dr. Tolson would have died the next year. He really strode the stage. His poetry readings were electrifying.

Here we are looking at *Dark Symphony* and Melvin is structuring this poem in movements. He has taken the history of black people through this poem into a certain crescendo, so as we get to the end we will advance, we will advance, we will advance. You can actually see how you would structure a choir behind there and do a choral poem. Even though his concepts were quite large, he was totally easy to understand. I don't mean simple. I just mean you could follow Dr. Tolson. He was talking to you; he never talked down to anybody. He didn't use words that you didn't understand, but he put together concepts that made you have to think.

I chose this particular poem because it is definitely a read-aloud. It is something that you'd like to have your class read aloud. Even if you are reading this book by yourself, if you read it aloud it is going to come alive in a way that hearing it in your head won't. It makes you say the words—and I guess, if Dr. Tolson hadn't been Dr. Tolson, he would have been Reverend Tolson, because he really has a cadence. It is a smooth cadence. And he wrote this outstanding poem about black Americans and how we have progressed in our dreams and our aspirations.

The Negro Speaks of Rivers

(TO W. E. B. DU BOIS)

I've known rivers:
I've known rivers ancient as the world and older than the
flow of human blood in human veins.

My soul has grown deep like the rivers.

I bathed in the Euphrates when dawns were young.
I built my hut near the Congo and it lulled me to sleep.
I looked upon the Nile and raised the pyramids above it.
I heard the singing of the Mississippi when Abe Lincoln
went down to New Orleans, and I've seen its muddy
bosom turn all golden in the sunset.

I've known rivers:
Ancient, dusky rivers.

My soul has grown deep like the rivers.

We're coming now to everybody's favorite writer, to my favorite and to everybody else's favorite, Langston Hughes. He
wrote *The Negro Speaks of Rivers* on his first trip across the
Mississippi on his way to visit his father in Mexico. It is such a
testament.

I know that we are taught that from dust we come and to dust we will go, yet there is something not quite . . . well . . . comfortable about that. Langston starts from what I believe is the logical thing; he starts with water.

Langston makes a claim for black Americans. He stakes our claim to civilization based on what we have known—rivers. Those waters of cities and commerce. Those waters that flow and overflow to take humans around the bend, in the words of the late writer Shiva Naipaul. And though we frequently speak of going to sea, it is actually a river we seek. The blues are a river that we ride down and paddle up.

I especially like Langston's dedication to Du Bois, who was urging young Negroes to speak of our people and do us proud. Du Bois had hoped that should we show imagination, the ability to conceptualize, perhaps something would be added to us that would force our oppressors to recognize that we are human . . . not just chattel capable of work, not just brutes who had to be controlled. It is a never-ending battle—the battle for the right to be called human—and Langston staked his claim on what we have always known: rivers.

We knew the first power not only of the moving waters but of the calming flow. We did not try to control the waters, we cuddled next to them and fell into an untroubled sleep. The slaves sang of the river Jordan as the deep river, using the Jordan as a metaphor for life and the crossing over as a passage to Heaven. The waters were also spoken of as cleansing, as "wade in the waters . . . God's going to trouble the waters." We in cities know water from a faucet—dripping down into our sinks, controlled, contained—not quite free. I wonder what Hughes would say if he lived in the city today. We know rivers; we sympathize with water. Everything wants to be free.

Dinner Guest: Me

I know I am
The Negro Problem
Being wined and dined,
Answering the usual questions
That come to white mind
Which seeks demurely
To probe in polite way
The why and wherewithal
Of darkness U.S.A.—
Wondering how things got this way
In current democratic night,
Murmuring gently
Over *fraises du bois,*
"I'm so ashamed of being white."

The lobster is delicious.
The wine divine,
And center of attention
At the damask table, mine.
To be a Problem on
Park Avenue at eight
Is not so bad.
Solutions to the Problem,
Of course, wait.

Langston is so wonderful because he looked at everything, no matter how large, no matter how small. "I know I am / The Negro Problem / Being wined and dined, / Answering the usual ques-

tions / That come to white mind." I love this poem because white
people used to do that. They did it during Langston's time and
mine.

People keep asking those stupid—"What does it feel like to
be black," "How does it feel to go to jail"—questions. Langston
was kinder than most so he found a wonderful sense of humor in
it. Some people got really tired of it. There's nothing to say, because it's a silly question. What does it feel like to be what,
homeless? What does it feel like to have AIDS? All of these
things, the one word is terrifying.

Langston looked at the world in a very joyful way. To say joyful is not to say that he was stupid. People tried to make Langston naive, as if he didn't really understand that the world is a
cruel place. Langston's father was a mean man and his mother
was a mentally delicate human being. I'm sure if anybody on
earth knew how difficult it is to be alive, Langston Hughes
knew. And yet he was always going to find a way to say there
must be something positive coming out of here. There must be
something that makes sense. "The lobster," he says, "is delicious. / The wine divine, / And center of attention / At the
damask table, mine." I just like the way that he approaches the
whole crazy situation.

You think about it when you get ready to go to college, or, if
you're in college, you think about it when your white colleagues,
your fellow students say things. At least when I was in school
they did, I shouldn't put it on you. When I was in school they
said things like "How do you get your hair to curl like that?"
The tendency was to answer, "Well, gee, I have bobby pins and I
pin it every night so that it will spring back so that I can have an
Afro." They would look at you with that rather ridiculous white
innocence that said, "Oh, really?" And you're just looking at
them like "Oh, please." I mean it is beyond stupidity. It's a certain meanness that somehow says that people can approach you
as if you are a fool, and you're expected to respond to that.

You're expected to be what they want you to be. Yet Langston
found a way to laugh.

Harlem

What happens to a dream deferred?

Does it dry up
like a raisin in the sun?
Or fester like a sore—
And then run?
Does it stink like rotten meat?
Or crust and sugar over—
like a syrupy sweet?

Maybe it just sags
Like a heavy load.

Or does it explode?

The poem *Harlem* is one of Langston's later poems. It is actually
the title poem of *Montage of a Dream Deferred,* but most people
know it by its first line, "What happens to a dream deferred?"
Lorraine Hansberry used a part of that poem, the phrase "a
raisin in the sun," as the title for her great play.

> *What happens to a dream deferred?*
> *Does it dry up*
> *like a raisin in the sun?*
> *Or fester like a sore—*
> *And then run?*

Langston was responding to riots in Harlem. As well it was time for riots. You push your people, you push your people, you push your people. Eventually the people are going to have to respond. Every time you read about a riot—I can't fight history in this or any other book—but every time you read about a riot it's always a case of some Negro somewhere *misunderstood* something. If they just hadn't misunderstood there wouldn't be this riot. They would have understood that the police were absolutely right to arrest the person, or the person they heard was being beaten or was being killed or had been killed, this wasn't really the case. If they had just gotten their communication right.

It makes you so angry because if we hadn't had a bad relationship, particularly with the police department—and that's in every city in the United States of America in terms of black Americans and white Americans—if our relationship with the police department wasn't what it is, then miscommunications would never occur.

So if ever there were people deserving of a riot, we probably are still. If we look at incidences compared to riots, I'm sure that the weight is still going to be on the side of black people. There have been more incidences that would call for a riot than there have been riots that called for incidences. It just drives you crazy. In Langston's day the people in Harlem had had it. They were tired of segregation. They were tired of people putting them down. They were tired of not being able to hold jobs where they lived. They were tired of people coming into their neighborhoods and taking everything that's good from them—taking their money, taking their dignity—and they rioted. It's not a question of why did they do that; it's a question of why did it take so long. The legendary patience of the Negro obviously was beginning to come to an end.

Dream Boogie

Good morning, daddy!
Ain't you heard
The boogie-woogie rumble
Of a dream deferred?

Listen closely:
You'll hear their feet
Beating out and beating out a—

    You think
    It's a happy beat?

Listen to it closely:
Ain't you heard
something underneath
like a—

    What did I say?

Sure,
I'm happy!
Take it away!

    Hey, pop!
    Re-bop!
    Mop!

    Y-e-a-h!

Langston Hughes spanned the Renaissance. His poem *The Negro Speaks of Rivers* really opened it, and the Renaissance goes on. Even right now there is no end. Langston is indelibly connected to all of us. One of the things that he did that was unusual was that he lived in Harlem all of his life. So he began to watch how Harlem changed from being a very nice neighborhood though, again, in many, many respects segregated, and in many, many respects overcrowded. At first it represented hope, and Langston watched that neighborhood that he loved, that community that he loved, just deliberately be turned into a slum. So he did a lot of variations on Harlem—you could call them his dream variations—and this is *Dream Boogie: Variation*.

Dream Boogie: Variation

Tinkling treble,
Rolling bass,
High noon teeth
In a midnight face,
Great long fingers
On great big hands,
Screaming pedals
Where his twelve-shoe lands,
Looks like his eyes
Are teasing pain,
A few minutes late
For the Freedom Train.

Same in Blues

I said to my baby,
Baby, take it slow.
I can't, she said, I can't!
I got to go!

>   *There's a certain*
>   *amount of traveling*
>   *in a dream deferred.*

Lulu said to Leonard,
I want a diamond ring.
Leonard said to Lulu,
You won't get a goddamn thing!

>   *A certain*
>   *amount of nothing*
>   *in a dream deferred.*

Daddy, daddy, daddy,
All I want is you.
You can have me, baby—
but my lovin' days is through.

>   *A certain*
>   *amount of impotence*
>   *in a dream deferred.*

Three parties
On my party line—
But that third party,
Lord, ain't mine!

> *There's liable*
> *to be confusion*
> *in a dream deferred.*

From river to river,
Uptown and down,
There's liable to be confusion
when a dream gets kicked around.

It's just absolutely positively clear what the American promise is, as long as it's been and as long as it will be: the American promise is always about a dream. It's always about the possibilities.

What America did and has done, and Langston is a pivotal artist on this, is they have finally said that black dreams may not apply. No black dreams here. You can put up with a lot. You can put up with an awful lot if you think somewhere down the line it's going to get better. To use the old spiritual, from the "sweet by and by," "we will understand it better by and by." Even if you don't know what that "by and by" will be, you can say there will be a better day. My great-grandmother, we called her Mamma Dear. Mamma Dear used to always say "never mind," and no matter what was going on—you didn't have something that you needed, your stockings had a hole or whatever, somebody called you a name—she said "never mind," and it's like one word, "n'mind," and you sort of understood, *never mind.* I can let it go. "Sticks and stones may break my bones, but words will never hurt me," and that's not true and we all know that. We actually know that we remember the words more than anything else. We remember the cruel things that people say to us more than anything else. You remember what somebody said to you in fifth or sixth grade. You remember what some teacher said to you, said that you were stupid or said you could never do whatever it was—you couldn't paint, you couldn't draw, you couldn't act, you couldn't be a cheerleader. It depends on when you came along. Whatever it was, somebody said you couldn't do it. Somebody said you were inadequate. And that's what you remember. You might remember that a schoolmate hit you or pushed you into the locker, but you remember the words much more than anything else.

I like Langston because he picked at things. He knew not just that he had a wonderful line, but he had a wonderful concept, the concept of "a dream deferred," because that is where America has punked out. America didn't punk out on its immigrants. America punked out on the Native Americans, and America definitely punked out on black Americans. And it is a dream, he said deferred, some would say never to be.

Martin Luther King came along and he said, "I still have a dream." But I think the beginning of that speech is more important than the end. "We are here to cash a check," King said. "I refuse to believe that the Bank of America is closed. We have a check that was written in 1619 and we're presenting it here for payment." I'm paraphrasing King. But King said more than nice words about children. He realizes that he is describing a dream, something that he looks forward to. Today, it's really clear that America is saying to its black citizens, "We're closing down that dream." But it's not just a dream, it's a right.

This country is a land mass that could be called anything, and for people to act like this is some kind of sacred territory is an insanity. It's just a bunch of people trying to live together, and if we're not going to be part of a dream of equality—a part of a dream of that which is the best of us, the idea that people help one another—if we're not going to do that, then this land mass doesn't any more deserve to be revered than anything else. All it is is where we are at this particular point, and it seems to me that it would be important and necessary that people respect not the reality but the concept, the dream of the possibilities. Langston brings that out better than anybody else.

Langston took it into blues. He took it into a boogie. He took it into variations on "a dream deferred." Our life is going to remain a variation on "a dream deferred" because we still have no possibility of joining together in any real sense. White America still does not care for its black citizens.

I, Too

I, too, sing America.

I am the darker brother.
They send me to eat in the kitchen
When company comes,
But I laugh,
And eat well,
And grow strong.

Tomorrow,
I'll be at the table
When company comes.
Nobody'll dare
Say to me,
"Eat in the kitchen,"
Then.   •

Besides,
They'll see how beautiful I am
And be ashamed—

I, too, am America.

Langston is trying to present the case that this is no way to treat
a people. He found us beautiful, and in doing so he thought
other people, if they would just look, would find us beautiful
also. Other people don't find us as beautiful as we wish they
would. I think that white Americans don't mind if we do something that pleases them, but the average white American and the
average black American, they don't have much truck with each
other. It's a shame because, as we know from *South Pacific,*
"You've got to be carefully taught to hate before you are six or
seven or eight." He is absolutely right in that we keep teaching
one another to hate. If the wages of sin are death, then certainly
the wages of hate are eternal damnation. You just cannot continue to hate.

If you read American history, and you see slavery and lynching and bombing federal buildings, you see white hatred. I think
that level of hatred needs to be examined. We're always asking,
Why are black people the way we are? My question is, What
makes white people the way they are? Every time black people
do something, everybody wants to study it. They want to study
Louis Farrakhan; they want to study Elijah Muhammad; they
want to study Malcolm X. Why do you people hate? We're not
the people that blow up the federal government. We're not the
people that shoot people down. We're not the people that lynch.
I think that somebody needs to study what makes these people
hate that way.

Dream Variations

To fling my arms wide
In some place of the sun,
To whirl and to dance
Till the white day is done.
Then rest at cool evening
Beneath a tall tree
While night comes on gently,
    Dark like me—
That is my dream!

To fling my arms wide
In the face of the sun,
Dance! Whirl! Whirl!
Till the quick day is done.
Rest at pale evening . . .
A tall, slim tree . . .
Night coming tenderly
    Black like me.

Langston is a very, very graceful writer. You actually can dance to Langston. He does a lot in three-quarter time. Langston was a simple writer, and he just did these jazz things. Langston had enough sense to see that this jazz, this music, was going to be terrifically important as time went on. This is jazz/dance/poetry.

Theme for English B

The instructor said,

> *Go home and write*
> *a page tonight.*
> *And let that page come out of you—*
> *Then, it will be true.*

I wonder if it's that simple?
I am twenty-two, colored, born in Winston-Salem.
I went to school there, then Durham, then here
to this college on the hill above Harlem.
I am the only colored student in my class.
The steps from the hill lead down into Harlem,
through a park, then I cross St. Nicholas,
Eighth Avenue, Seventh, and I come to the Y,
the Harlem Branch Y, where I take the elevator
up to my room, sit down, and write this page:

It's not easy to know what is true for you or me
at twenty-two, my age. But I guess I'm what
I feel and see and hear, Harlem, I hear you:
hear you, hear me—we two—you, me, talk on this page.
(I hear New York, too.) Me—who?
Well, I like to eat, sleep, drink, and be in love.
I like to work, read, learn, and understand life.
I like a pipe for a Christmas present,
or records—Bessie, bop, or Bach.
I guess being colored doesn't make me *not* like
the same things other folks like who are other races.

So will my page be colored that I write?
Being me, it will not be white.
But it will be
a part of you, instructor.
You are white—
yet a part of me, as I am a part of you.
That's American.
Sometimes perhaps you don't want to be a part of me.
Nor do I often want to be a part of you.
But we are, that's true!
As I learn from you,
I guess you learn from me—
although you're older—and white—
and somewhat more free.

This is my page for English B.

Theme for English B is one of my favorites. It is really lovely. I like that line, "I like to . . . be in love" because at twenty-two one does like to be in love. That's what makes twenty-two charming. By the time you get to be forty-two it makes it stupid, but at twenty-two it's wonderful.

Notes on the Broadway Theatre

You've done taken my blues and gone—
Sure have! You sing 'em on Broadway,
And you sing 'em in Hollywood Bowl.
You mixed 'em up with symphonies,
And you fixed 'em so they don't sound like me.
Yep, you done taken my blues and gone!
You also took my spirituals and gone.
Now you've rocked-and-rolled 'em to death!
You put me in *Macbeth,*
In *Carmen Jones,* and *Anna Lucasta,*
And all kinds of *Swing Mikados*
And in everything but what's about me—
But someday somebody'll
Stand up and talk about me,
And write about me—
Black and beautiful—
And sing about me,
And put on plays about me!
I reckon it'll be me myself!
Yes, it'll be me.

Langston drank deeply from the sources around him. I'm so happy he didn't stay in Kansas, or Durham for that matter. Nothing against Winston-Salem and Durham. I just think it's so good that he got to an urban area so that he could really look around and see what our people were doing. *Macbeth, Carmen Jones, Anna Lucasta, Swing Mikado,* these were just plays with black casts that were popular. Here Langston is commenting on the use of black people in the Broadway theater of his time.

I only knew one person, though, who ever had a bad story about Langston Hughes and that was Alice Childress. Alice Childress is the author of *One in the Family* and *A Hero Ain't Nothin but a Sandwich*. She did some beautiful books and she is a wonderful writer. Alice was married to Alvin Childress, who played Amos in *Amos and Andy*. Alice was a race woman. They used to call them race women. She told Childress that if he continued to play Amos she was going to leave him, and he said it was a job and he was going to continue to do that. She did divorce him, though she kept his name, Childress, for the rest of her life.

When Alice first got to New York she was a pretty young woman. Like most young people, she wanted to meet Langston Hughes and she finally ran him down at the Y. At that point he was having a reading, and she asked him if he would look at some of her poetry. All of the stories that I ever heard about Langston said that Langston had no ability to say no, so he agreed to meet her. Langston was still a young man, he lived in a four-story walk-up in Harlem. He agreed to meet her at one o'clock, and she went over to his house.

I knew Ms. Childress to be a very punctual woman. So she went over to the house and she started walking up the stairs when she heard the door slam and she heard Langston's voice, and he was saying to a friend of his, "Hurry up, we've got to get out of here. I promised this girl that I would look at her poems and she'll be here any minute." Alice Childress stepped back into the shadows and they went bounding downstairs laughing about something else and went on about their business.

She never forgave him. I saw it differently, and I told her that. "Didn't it occur to you, Alice," I said, "that maybe he didn't want to read your poetry?" It is so unfair, because perfect strangers accost you and you're trying to do what you're trying to do, and you're trying to be a nice person about it, and they say to you, "I want you to read my poetry and tell me whether or not I have talent." Well, clearly Ms. Childress had talent because she went on to a great publishing career; she got a lot of work done. He just didn't want to read it.

I was kind of glad to hear it, because I had heard so many wonderful stories about Langston Hughes that I just thought, "Oh, he's got to be human, he's got to get tired sometimes, he's got to be sick of all of it at some point." Langston worked very hard at not letting any despairing things come. "Where never is heard a discouraging word," he used to say all the time.

Langston always kept looking, he kept looking, and he was fascinated by and he simply loved the energy and the fortitude of black people. He did not despair. He understood that, sure, there were things that could be done better, and that a lot of things had been done to us that needed to be addressed, but there was also always strength, and beauty, and life.

ARNA BONTEMPS (1902–1973)

A Black Man Talks of Reaping

I have sown beside all waters in my day.
I planted deep within my heart the fear
that wind or fowl would take the grain away.
I planted safe against this stark, lean year.

I scattered seed enough to plant the land
in rows from Canada to Mexico.
but for my reaping only what the hand
can hold at once is all that I can show.

Yet what I sowed and what the orchard yields
my brother's sons are gathering stalk and root;
small wonder then my children glean in fields
they have not sown, and feed on bitter fruit.

When I was at Fisk University it was probably just the best time
to be at Fisk. We were very fortunate in that the English department had Leslie Collins, who is still with us. Dr. Collins is still at
Fisk, he is a wonderful poet and an expert on the Harlem Renaissance. We had Robert Hayden, who is one of the great poets
of America, and we had Aaron Douglas in the art department.
Mr. Douglas was very kind. We had Arna Bontemps at the head
of the library. Mr. Bontemps was a good-looking guy. I remember one day rushing across the quad. Fisk has a beautiful physical plant and Erasmus Hall is in the middle of the quad. I

remember rushing across the quad and just running smack-dab into, not physically, but getting right there in front of Mr. Bontemps. I said, "Hi, how are you, Dr. Bontemps." And he said, "I'm fine, how are you?" He didn't know me from a hole in the wall. My day was made.

Arna is a good writer and he and Langston were definitely brothers under the skin. They were good friends. They really got along. I wanted to include one of my favorites of Dr. Bontemps's poems, *A Black Man Talks of Reaping*.

I have sown beside all waters in my day.
I planted deep within my heart the fear
that wind or fowl would take the grain away.
I planted safe against the stark, lean year.

He is talking about more than slavery. He is describing the emotional gathering, the emotional planting that we do.

I scattered seed enough to plant the land
in rows from Canada to Mexico.

Now that could be any number of things. That could be wheat or that could be people.

but for my reaping only what the hand
can hold at once is all that I can show.

That's today's migrant workers—any migrant worker could write this poem because they, too, have sown and they have reaped, and yet all they get is what they can immediately deal with, there's no residue there.

Yet, what I sold and what the orchard yields
my brother's sons are gathering stalk and root;
small wonder then my children glean in fields
they have not sown, and feed on bitter fruit.

To be black is to always have something taken away from you.

Heritage

(FOR HAROLD JACKMAN)

What is Africa to me:
Copper sun or scarlet sea,
Jungle star or jungle track,
Strong bronzed men, or regal black
Women from whose loins I sprang
When the birds of Eden sang?
One three centuries removed
From the scenes his fathers loved,
Spicy grove, cinnamon tree,
What is Africa to me?

So I lie, who all day long
Want no sound except the song
Sung by wild barbaric birds
Goading, massive jungle herds,
Juggernauts of flesh that pass
Trampling tall defiant grass
Where young forest lovers lie,
Plighting troth beneath the sky.
So I lie, who always hear,
Though I cram against my ear
Both my thumbs, and keep them there,
Great drums throbbing through the air.

So I lie, whose fount of pride,
Dear distress, and joy allied,
Is my somber flesh and skin,
With the dark blood dammed within
Like great pulsing tides of wine
That, I fear, must burst the fine
Channels of the chafing net
Where they surge and foam and fret.

Africa? A book one thumbs
Listlessly, till slumber comes.
Unremembered are her bats
Circling through the night, her cats
Crouching in the river reeds,
Stalking gentle flesh that feeds
By the river brink; no more
Does the bugle-throated roar
Cry that monarch claws have leapt
From the scabbards where they slept.
Silver snakes that once a year
Doff the lovely coats you wear,
Seek no covert in your fear
Lest a mortal eye should see;
What's your nakedness to me?
Here no leprous flowers rear
Fierce corollas in the air;
Here no bodies sleek and wet,
Dripping mingled rain and sweat,
Tread the savage measures of
Jungle boys and girls in love.

What is last year's snow to me,
Last year's anything? The tree
Budding yearly must forget
How its past arose or set—
Bough and blossom, flower, fruit,
Even what shy bird with mute
Wonder at her travail there,
Meekly labored in its hair.
One three centuries removed
From the scenes his father loved,
Spicy grove, cinnamon tree,
What is Africa to me?

So I lie, who find no peace
Night or day, no slight release
From the unremittent beat
Made by cruel padded feet
Walking through my body's street.
Up and down they go, and back,
Treading out a jungle track.
So I lie, who never quite
Safely sleep from rain at night—
I can never rest at all
When the rain begins to fall;
Like a soul gone mad with pain
I must match its weird refrain;
Ever must I twist and squirm,
Writhing like a baited worm,
While its primal measures drip
Through my body, crying, "Strip!
Doff this new exuberance.

Come and dance the Lover's Dance!"
In an old remembered way
Rain works on me night and day.

Quaint, outlandish heathen gods
Black men fashion out of rods,
Clay, and brittle bits of stone,
In a likeness like their own,
My conversion came high-priced;
I belong to Jesus Christ,
Preacher of humility;
Heathen gods are naught to me.

Father, Son, and Holy Ghost,
So I make an idle boast;
Jesus of the twice-turned cheek,
Lamb of God, although I speak
With my mouth thus, in my heart,
Do I play a double part.
Ever at Thy glowing altar
Must my heart grow sick and falter,
Wishing He I served were black,
Thinking then it would not lack
Precedent of pain to guide it,
Let who would or might deride it;
Surely then this flesh would know
Yours had borne a kindred woe.
Lord, I fashion dark gods, too,
Daring even to give You
Dark despairing features where,
Crowned with dark rebellious hair,

Patience wavers just so much as
Mortal grief compels, while touches
Quick and hot, of anger, rise
To smitten cheek and weary eyes.
Lord, forgive me if my need
Sometimes shapes a human creed.

All day long and all night through,
One thing only must I do:
Quench my pride and cool my blood,
Lest I perish in the flood.
Lest a hidden ember set
Timber that I thought was wet
Burning like the dryest flax,
Melting like the merest wax,
Lest the grave restore its dead.
Not yet has my heart or head
In the least way realized
They and I are civilized.

Countee Cullen was a great writer who has never really had his
fair share. America has not given him any kind of due. I know
that black Americans do. He, like Arna Bontemps, like Langston Hughes, like Jean Toomer, like many, many others, heeded
the admonition that we should look to our African past to find
out what it is that can inform our present. Countee fell right
back into the Renaissance, right smack-dab into it. The wonderful thing about Countee is that he taught James Baldwin, and
that's a true link, a connection.

He looked reflectively at himself and at his people.

What is Africa to me:
Copper sun or scarlet sea,
Jungle star or jungle track,
Strong bronzed men, or regal black
Women from whose loins I sprang
When the birds of Eden sang?

One of the things that he wants to do is trace all of Africa, trace the African civilization. He also wants to trace where he is, and how he can respond, and what he has to do in order to be able to control his rage—control the way that he has been treated, the way he was snatched from his birthplace, from the land not of his physical birth, but, of course, of his ancestors' birth.

All day long and all night through,
One thing only must I do:
Quench my pride and cool my blood,
Lest I perish in the flood.

Countee is trying to deal with Africa as closed. He will not go to Africa. He will not even see the continent in his lifetime. I just assume that the spirit of Countee Cullen would fly away and see whatever he wants. But he tried to look at the continent. He looked at it in respect.

Countee Cullen is conceded to be one of the really great minds of his time, not just of the Renaissance, but actually of his time. He wrote some of the most remarkable poems.

Yet Do I Marvel

I doubt not God is good, well-meaning, kind.
And did He stoop to quibble could tell why
The little buried mole continues blind,
Why flesh that mirrors Him must some day die,
Make plain the reason tortured Tantalus
Is baited by the fickle fruit, declare
If merely brute caprice dooms Sisyphus
To struggle up a never-ending stair.
Inscrutable His ways are, and immune
To catechism by a mind too strewn
With petty cares to slightly understand
What awful brain compels His awful hand.
Yet do I marvel at this curious thing:
To make a poet black, and bid him sing!

I'm sure deep down he didn't marvel, because deep down he knew very well that he is a poet who is black and who sings very well. But we have this angst, I suppose is the word, this sort of sigh to say, "I wonder why."

When you think of Countee Cullen, first and foremost, he was married to Yolande Du Bois. Perhaps old Doc Du Bois thought that the most brilliant of the Renaissance men should be kin to him, and Doc Du Bois had lost his son. His son had died shortly before his first birthday, so the loss of his son meant that Du Bois was looking for an intellectual heir, and I'm sure he found Countee Cullen quite worthy. There is not much said about the marriage. We know that it didn't work, but I would imagine being the son-in-law of Dr. Du Bois is not one of the easy things.

Incident

(FOR ERIC WALROND)

Once riding in old Baltimore,
    Heart-filled, head-filled with glee,
I saw a Baltimorean
    Keep looking straight at me.

Now I was eight and very small,
    And he was no whit bigger,
And so I smiled, but he poked out
    His tongue and called me, "Nigger."

I saw the whole of Baltimore
    From May until December;
Of all the things that happened there
    That's all that I remember.

Countee Cullen wrote a signature poem in many respects, called *Incident*. It's a poem that we used to hear in church. People recited that at the Sunday school talent shows. People would recite poetry, a lot of Paul Laurence Dunbar. But almost invariably *Incident* was recited.

As a little kid you have to be, as we wrote earlier, carefully taught to hate. A little kid sitting on a bus looking at another little kid would do what any other kid would do under those circumstances, smile. And the little white kid is learning, he's learning already, "I must hate, I must hate."

Countee wrote *Three Epitaphs,* one for his grandmother, one for Paul Laurence Dunbar, and one "For a Lady I Know." The one "For a Lady I Know" is quite cynical:

For a Lady I Know

She even thinks that up in heaven
Her class lies late and snores,
While poor black cherubs rise at seven
To do celestial chores.

I'm sure that that's a fact.

For Paul Laurence Dunbar

Born of the sorrowful of heart
Mirth was a crown upon his head;
Pride kept his twisted lips apart
In jest, to hide a heart that bled.

That's quite true. Dunbar was a deep thinker and a caring man, and people tried, as they often do, to use his gifts against him.

For My Grandmother

This lovely flower fell to seed;
Work gently sun and rain;
She held it as her dying creed
That she would grow again.

And of course she did. His grandmother grew through him. There is just nothing not to like about Countee Cullen. He is a person determined to have a voice. Countee was an orphan and he was adopted by Reverend Cullen. For some reason, after the thirties, he never did write anymore. That was our loss. He was a young man when he died. You really do wish that Countee had been able to live much longer, had been able to do more.

Sonnet to a Negro in Harlem

You are disdainful and magnificent—
Your perfect body and your pompous gait,

Your dark eyes flashing solemnly with hate,
Small wonder that you are incompetent
To imitate those whom you so despise—
Your shoulders towering high above the throng,
Your head thrown back in rich, barbaric song,
Palm trees and mangoes stretched before your eyes.
Let others toil and sweat for labor's sake
And wring from grasping hands their meed of gold.
Why urge ahead your supercilious feet?
Scorn will efface each footprint that you make.
I love your laughter arrogant and bold.
You are too splendid for this city street.

Helene Johnson is one of the few women in the Renaissance.
Jessie Fauset is very, very important because she is the one who
did all of the editing. Everybody knows Zora Neale Hurston.
Dorothy West—her cousin—is still alive, and Helene died quite
recently. Helene wrote *Sonnet to a Negro in Harlem.*

In many respects this poem is in line with—not an echo, don't
misunderstand—but it's related to Countee Cullen's refrain
"What Is Africa to Me." It links well with Waring Cuney's *No
Images.* Helene Johnson's poem is to a young black man. Waring's is to a young black woman.

No Images

She does not know
Her beauty,
She thinks her brown body
Has no glory.

If she could dance
Naked,
Under palm trees
And see her image in the river
She would know.

But there are no palm trees
On the street,
And dish water gives back no images.

No *Images* is an outstanding poem because it's true, and it's true not only of black women, but it is true of women period. You wonder sometimes why poor white women sit in these trailer camps thinking of themselves as ugly and being afraid. You look at a poor woman in South Carolina who murders her boys for whatever reason. To kill your children is to be out of options. You must have looked at dishwater and seen no images; the same way that the girl in the poem had to look at dishwater; the same way that Mammy had to look at it in *Gone with the Wind;* the same way that we all do—except that now, of course, what we do is we put everything in the dishwashing machine, and we run our electric bill up by having the dishes washed, and I say good for us, because at least we don't have to sit there and contemplate who we are.

I do, though, know for a fact that both Toni Morrison and Alice Walker liked to wash dishes because they liked to think, and they both have given interviews saying, "Well, I like to wash dishes because it helps me think." Me, I don't. I used to. When I was little I had a job, my first job in fact, for our next-door neighbors, Aunt Lil and Uncle Rich. Aunt Lil paid me fifty cents a week and I would wash her dishes, because that was not like real dishes. I mean, she and Uncle Rich would probably have a cup of coffee and a glass of juice in the morning, and I would go after school and wash their dishes every day, and I would get my fifty cents.

I remember liking Aunt Lil's kitchen. All of the houses were exactly alike, but she would keep the radio going all the time. I remember hearing the music while I was there and I'd wash the dishes, and I like soap. I've always liked soap, and I think she probably went broke with just the amount of soap I would use to wash two cups, two saucers, and probably two glasses.

I don't have any bad feelings about washing dishes; I just don't do it, and I'm really happy that the dishwashing machine came in. But for those budding young novelists out there and future Nobelists, I think probably what you want is to do what Toni Morrison did and do what the best did, and Toni's the best and she washed dishes. And Alice is very good and she washed dishes. So perhaps you won't want a dishwasher.

⟶ Richard Wright (1908–1960)

Between the World and Me

And one morning while in the woods I stumbled suddenly
    upon the thing,
Stumbled upon it in a grassy clearing guarded by scaly
    oaks and elms.
And the sooty details of the scene rose, thrusting
    themselves between the world and me. . . .

There was a design of white bones slumbering forgottenly
    upon a cushion of ashes.
There was a charred stump of a sapling pointing a blunt
    finger accusingly at the sky.
There were torn tree limbs, tiny veins of burnt leaves, and
    a scorched coil of greasy hemp;
A vacant shoe, an empty tie, a ripped shirt, a lonely hat,
    and a pair of trousers stiff with black blood.
And upon the trampled grass were buttons, dead matches,
    butt-ends of cigars and cigarettes, peanut shells, a
    drained gin-flask, and a whore's lipstick;
Scattered traces of tar, restless arrays of feathers, and the
    lingering smell of gasoline.
And through the morning air the sun poured yellow
    surprise into the eye sockets of a stony skull. . . .
And while I stood my mind was frozen with a cold pity for
    the life that was gone.
The ground gripped my feet and my heart was circled by
    icy walls of fear—

The sun died in the sky; a night wind muttered in the
    grass and fumbled the leaves in the trees; the woods
    poured forth the hungry yelping of hounds; the
    darkness screamed with thirsty voices; and the
    witnesses rose and lived;
The dry bones stirred, rattled, lifted, melting themselves
    into my bones.
The grey ashes formed flesh firm and black, entering into
    my flesh.
The gin-flask passed from mouth to mouth; cigars and
    cigarettes glowed, the whore smeared lipstick red
    upon her lips,
And a thousand faces swirled around me, clamoring that
    my life be burned. . . .

And then they had me, stripped me, battering my teeth
    into my throat till I swallowed my own blood.
My voice was drowned in the roar of their voices, and my
    black wet body slipped and rolled in their hands as
    they bound me to the sapling.
And my skin clung to the bubbling hot tar, falling from
    me in limp patches.
And the down and quills of the white feathers sank into
    my raw flesh, and I moaned in my agony.
Then my blood was cooled mercifully, cooled by a
    baptism of gasoline.
And in a blaze of red I leaped to the sky as pain rose like
    water, boiling my limbs.
Panting, begging I clutched childlike, clutched to the hot
    sides of death.
Now I am dry bones and my face a stony skull staring in
    yellow surprise at the sun. . . .

Richard Wright was the author of *Native Son, Eight Men, Pagan Spain, Black Power, Uncle Tom's Children*. He was a premier novelist and essayist, probably one of America's first truly angry black young men, and clearly a forerunner of the existential movement. He was the outsider. He was an existentialist in that he and his characters constantly created themselves by the events as they occurred. He ended up being very comfortable with French intellectuals like Jean-Paul Sartre and Albert Camus when he finally migrated to Europe, when he finally got sick of America. I chose his poem *Between the World and Me* because it is probably prototypically not only Richard Wright but prototypically what it is with America and black people.

> And one morning while in the woods I stumbled sud-
> denly upon the thing,
> Stumbled upon it in a grassy clearing guarded by scaly
> oaks and elms.
> And the sooty details of the scene rose, thrusting them-
> selves between the world and me. . . .

He is not using "between the world and me" as "this is between us"; he is using it as "this is a barrier." Lynching is a barrier between black Americans and the rest of America. Lynching will always be a barrier.

Wright is looking at the skull, the dead remains of somebody, somebody who was burned, who was lynched, who was tortured, who was whipped, who had gasoline thrown in the wounds, who was then burned and whose only release was going to be death. It's not right. It is not right to put people in that position.

Richard Wright had written a lot about lynching. Everybody wrote about lynching because on the average from 1909 to I think 1918, on the average a black person was lynched every week. In 1964 when they were looking for the bodies of the murdered civil rights workers Michael (Mickey) Schwerner, James Chaney, and Andrew Goodman, they found a number of other bodies in various places in various states of decay. Nobody asked, How did this happen? Ten years previous to that, in searching for the body of Emmett Till, there were at least four known cases of bodies that were located in and around Tallahatchie. Again, once it was determined that this body was not the body of Emmett Till, it was simply sent to a colored undertaker. These four bodies were sent to a colored undertaker. The old gospel song talks about "many thousand gone." Somebody says, "Nobody knows but Jesus" how many people were taken in the night. What were we going to do, call the sheriff? The sheriff was the one who was taking them. Who were you going to complain to?

When the police belong to racist groups, it amounts to having a group of Jews being guarded by Nazis. We know that the effect of that is not just that the Jews are not going to be properly guarded. They are going to be tortured. They are going to be sexually abused. They are going to be anything else that the depths of the human mind can take itself to.

I do wonder sometimes, I do wonder what it is about the human mind that goes to pain and degradation. I do wonder what it is. We talk about original sin. We talk about ignorance. We talk about people not having had a chance. We talk about poverty—a bunch of things—but there is something not quite right about the human species, because, given half a chance, we'd be eating one another.

I don't know why crowds of people gather to torture people. I would have had a hard time. I think, me, I would have had a hard time even back when they stoned people. Even back in those old days where we didn't like what somebody did so "We are going to stone you." Well, damn, you don't have to like it. What kind of craziness is it—that makes people pick up a rock and say, "I'm going to stone you to death?"

I think that race has no truck here. I think that, in reality, there is something wrong with human beings, and unless we are willing to face the fact that something is really wrong with human beings, unless we are willing to face the fact that somewhere in our imaginations we are evil, vicious people, it is not going to work.

This is standing between not just Richard Wright and the world but between all of us and the world. This idea that you can hunt down a human being, tie up his hands and his feet, and just proceed to torture him, the end result being death. It is not even that you are trying to kill him, because if you were trying to kill him, you could have shot him. You could have done it a lot easier. What you are trying to do is put him in a lot of pain. What kind of sense does that make? That doesn't make any sense to me.

Wright says, "Now I am dry bones." Here he took on the persona of the lynched man. "Now I am dry bones and my face a stony skull staring in / yellow surprise at the sun. . . ." Whether he experienced this in his mind, or whether he experienced it in reality, that level of horror will make a stony skull out of anybody. It will drive you crazy. When you consider that to be in Mississippi when Wright grew up was to be so marginal anyway, it just cannot be surprising that he did not write comedy, he wasn't going to be a Langston Hughes. He was not going to find a way to love despite it all. Richard Wright was going to be very upset, and he was going to go through his life being very upset, because life had shown him that it will not be kind to him.

Life had shown Wright that, if given a chance, the crowds will come and scream for Barabbas. He could have called his poem "Give Us Barabbas," because if you can get Barabbas down, then that means you have room to torture Jesus. Wright's poem is very powerful, a very hard poem to read. It gives you bad dreams, and yet it says so much about who human beings are, who we have been, and, since I am hopeful, I hope it doesn't say who we will become.

There was a wonderful woman, who died probably in the late seventies, named Anna Hedgeman. Mrs. Hedgeman was a Fiskite. She came to visit our history class and she gave an outstanding, lively lecture. Mrs. Hedgeman was—I guess the cliché term would be—a spry old lady. Her talk was about Abraham Lincoln and the Emancipation Proclamation and how it came to be. Mrs. Hedgeman said she had always wanted to make a change in the Lincoln Memorial, which features a statue of Lincoln sitting on a chair. She wanted to see a big statue of Frederick Douglass standing behind the seated Lincoln, guiding his hand to sign the Emancipation Proclamation.

I always thought that would be really neat if black people ever got control of the United States we would, of course, tear down some of the statues because we just don't like them . . . like all of Richmond would probably not have a statue standing. Once we got over that and we would look at the bigger documents, the bigger monuments, the important things we are still going to adhere to, one of which has to be Lincoln. It would be really super to commission someone, an Ed Dwight for instance, to do a strong Frederick Douglass leaning over Abraham Lincoln.

Frederick Douglass

When it is finally ours, this freedom, this liberty, this
        beautiful
and terrible thing, needful to man as air,
usable as earth; when it belongs at last to all,
when it is truly instinct, brain matter, diastole, systole,

reflex action; when it is finally won; when it is more
than the gaudy mumbo jumbo of the politicians:
this man, this Douglass, this former slave, this Negro
beaten to his knees, exiled, visioning a world
where none is lonely, none hunted, alien,
this man, superb in love and logic, this man
shall be remembered. Oh, not with statues' rhetoric,
not with legends and poems and wreaths of bronze alone,
but with the lives grown out of his life, the lives
fleshing his dream of the beautiful, needful thing.

Robert Hayden's *Frederick Douglass* is a beautiful poem. He
talks about "When it is finally ours, this freedom, this liberty,
this beautiful / and terrible thing, needful to man as air, / usable
as earth; when it belongs at last to all."

He is just saying that human freedom is not one of the things
that has frightened him. He is saying Frederick Douglass won't
have a statue. We probably will not raise any monuments, but
that our lives will be a monumental aspect of Frederick Douglass, "this former slave, this Negro," as he said, "visioning a
world."

Frederick Douglass was a powerful man. He realized that a
people will get exactly what they will take, and he is right about
that. Frederick Douglass was an exceptional man, too. He
changed how people saw the world. What was intolerable to
him was that others could not envision another way. I never saw
that Douglass was as arrogant as Du Bois and I never saw that he
was as short-tempered, that he was impatient with people who
thought differently and who did not have the same response to
life and its responsibilities as he. But he was very clear about

what the possibilities were, what the probabilities were, and if
you wanted to be free what the price was that you were going to
have to pay. He turned himself into that which was possible, he
defined the limits of possibility. He became an advocate and a
spokesperson. He was a good person. He became a great agitator for this freedom, this "terrible thing, needful to man as air, /
usable as earth," and what he urged people to do was to seize
that moment, to seize the freedom.

Robert Hayden was at Fisk University with us, and Dr. Hayden had glasses that looked like Popsicles. He was very nice, and
he wore bow ties. He always wore bow ties. It seemed to me that
Dr. Hayden took short steps. Aaron Douglas would hunch his
shoulders and you would see him striding across campus, and
Dr. Bontemps was always busy. He seemed quick, but it seemed
like Dr. Hayden always took little steps, as if he didn't want to
offend anybody or hurt anybody but he just wanted to get where
he was going.

Those Winter Sundays

Sundays too my father got up early
and put his clothes on in the blueblack cold,
then with cracked hands that ached
from labor in the weekday weather made
banked fires blaze. No one ever thanked him.

I'd wake and hear the cold splintering, breaking.
When the rooms were warm, he'd call,
and slowly I would rise and dress,
fearing the chronic angers of that house,

Speaking indifferently to him,
who had driven out the cold
and polished my good shoes as well.
What did I know, what did I know
of love's austere and lonely offices?

One of my favorite and one of my mother's favorite poems is *Those Winter Sundays*. This poem is set in the days of coal stoves and fireplaces. Hayden was born in 1913, and I think of my mother having different memories of her father because Grandpapa never raised his voice to anybody. There were no chronic angers at 400 Mulvaney. My mother was born in 1917, so she and Mr. Hayden were not that far apart. They were both very much aware of someone making the cold go away, making it a little more comfortable for them to arise and do what they should do, which in his case was study as well as in my mother's. Their generation was always going to go to school, they were expected to go to school, they began to embody the dreams of a people.

The Whipping

The old woman across the way
   is whipping the boy again
and shouting to the neighborhood
   her goodness and his wrongs.   •

Wildly he crashes through elephant ears,
    pleads in dusty zinnias,
while she in spite of crippling fat
    pursues and corners him.

She strikes and strikes the shrilly circling
    boy till the stick breaks
in her hand. His tears are rainy weather
    to woundlike memories:

My head gripped in bony vise
    of knees, the writhing struggle
to wrench free, the blows, the fear
    worse than blows that hateful

Words could bring, the face that I
    no longer knew or loved . . .
Well, it is over now, it is over,
    and the boy sobs in his room,

And the woman leans muttering against
    a tree, exhausted, purged—
avenged in part for lifelong hidings
    she has had to bear.

The Whipping is a wonderful poem. "The old woman across the way / is whipping the boy again / and shouting to the neighborhood / her goodness and his wrongs." What she is actually doing is trying to pre-whip him, so that when life comes and whips him again he will already be aware that he can withstand it. She wants to make him a strong man by showing him now, as he is a boy, now you have to withstand this. He is running around shrieking, and both of them are appealing to the neighbors, but the reality is she is trying to show him, if I do this then you will be all right, and if you are all right, then I will have done my job.

Runagate Runagate

I.

Runs falls rises stumbles on from darkness into darkness
and the darkness thicketed with shapes of terror
and the hunters pursuing and the hounds pursuing
and the night cold and the night long and the river
to cross and the jack-muh-lanterns beckoning beckoning
and blackness ahead and when shall I reach that
     somewhere
morning and keep on going and never turn back and keep
     on going

    Runagate
        Runagate
            Runagate

Many thousands rise and go
many thousands crossing over

        O mythic North
      O star-shaped yonder Bible city

Some go weeping and some rejoicing
some in coffins and some in carriages
some in silks and some in shackles

             Rise and go or fare you well

No more auction block for me
no more driver's lash for me

        If you see my Pompey, 30 yrs of age,
        new breeches, plain stockings, negro shoes;
        if you see my Anna, likely young mulatto
        branded E on the right cheek, R on the left,
        catch them if you can and notify subscriber.
        Catch them if you can, but it won't be easy.
        They'll dart underground when you try to catch
            them,
        plunge into quicksand, whirlpools, mazes,
        turn into scorpions when you try to catch them.

And before I'll be a slave
I'll be buried in my grave

        North star and bonanza gold
        I'm bound for the freedom, freedom-bound
        and oh Susyanna don't you cry for me

             Runagate

             Runagate

II.

Rises from their anguish and their power,

  Harriet Tubman,

  woman of the earth, whipscarred,
  a summoning, a shining

  Mean to be free

And this was the way of it, brethren brethren,
way we journeyed from Can't to Can.
Moon so bright and no place to hide,
the cry up and the patterollers riding,
hound dogs belling in bladed air
And fear starts a-murbling, Never make it,
we'll never make it. *Hush that now,*
and she's turned upon us, levelled pistol
glinting in the moonlight:
Dead folks can't jaybird-talk, she says;
you keep on going now or die, she says.

Wanted   Harriet Tubman   alias The General
alias Moses   Stealer of Slaves

In league with Garrison   Alcott   Emerson
Garrett   Douglass   Thoreau   John Brown

Armed and known to be Dangerous

Wanted   Reward   Dead or Alive

Tell me, Ezekiel, oh tell me do you see
mailed Jehovah coming to deliver me?

Hoot-owl calling in the ghosted air,
five times calling to the hants in the air.
Shadow of a face in the scary leaves,
shadow of a voice in the talking leaves:
　　　Come ride-a my train

　　Oh that train, ghost-story train
　　through swamp and savanna movering movering,
　　over trestles of dew, through caves of the wish,
　　Midnight Special on a sabre track movering movering,
　　first stop Mercy and the last Hallelujah.

　　Come ride-a my train

　　　Mean mean mean to be free.

Mr. Hayden wrote many great poems, but outstanding are *Middle Passage* and *Runagate Runagate*. I know this about Mr. Hayden: He wrote this poem, I think in 1948, and really thought that it could be perfected. He continued to work on *Runagate* until the day he died. There are many different versions of it. He just kept scratching at it. He just kept moving things around to make a more perfect poem. He is going to use spirituals in here. "And before I'll be a slave/I'll be buried in my grave." He is going to use folklore; he is going to use description. He is going to change voices a million times; he is going to try to show how the run-away had to look at the world.

What he is saying—and I appreciate it a lot because I got tired of hearing that black people were just really happy to be slaves and every now and then Harriet Tubman would come along and force a few of them out of slavery—is that there was a movement. People wanted to get out of slavery, and running was one of the ways. There were not a whole lot of stories about slaves running away from Georgia, or slaves running away from Alabama, or slaves running away from Mississippi—and certainly not going north to Mississippi, because there is no place north to go. If you go south you end up in New Orleans, and I am sure there were more Mississippi slaves that ended up in New Orleans than we know. When you get that far south you are not likely to be successful. But if you were a Kentucky slave, if you were a slave in Maryland, if you were a slave in Virginia, you had every opportunity. You were not always going to make it, but there was a lot of running. People ran because it was close enough that you could begin to see that there was salvation, there was possibility.

The Underground Railroad was a totally wonderful concept. The Quakers were very much a part of it because they were against slavery and they built their homes and provided shelter, and they had false gates, false floors, false doors. They did a lot so that they could help move the slaves. The slaves fled all the way up into Nova Scotia, into Canada, and as the commercial says, "We judge success one investor at a time," the Underground Railroad movement judged success one slave at a time.

There were many children involved in the Underground Railroad, but there were more adults involved in running because children are unreliable. There were more adults involved because an adult could count on himself. Tubman convinced people that they were going to be free or they were going to be dead. She was right; there was no point in letting everybody else go down because somebody got scared. There are times in life when there is a contract, I suppose you could say, if you were a law student. The time to punk out on the contract is before you go. Once you take that one step off the plantation, then you are committed to being free or being dead, because anything short of that is going to endanger everybody else and everybody else would have to be a fool to let you slip up. Hayden's poem conducts the railroad. It reads very well:

> *Runs falls rises stumbles on from darkness into darkness*
> *and the darkness thicketed with shapes of terror*
> *and the hunters pursuing and the hounds pursuing*
> *and the night cold and the night long and the river*
> *to cross and the jack-muh-laterns beckoning beckoning*
> *blackness ahead and when shall I reach that*
> *somewhere*
> *morning and keep on going and never turn back and*
>   *keep*
> *on going*

He is showing that a slave owner can actually turn around and say things like "a stealer of slaves," as if they haven't stolen the person. Mississippi recently, and recently being 1994, finally ratified the Thirteenth Amendment and agreed that the Civil War was over and the black people are free. I'm talking 1994. So you know it is kind of time that people got caught up. It's a shame that we are still looking at a world that can use those kinds of concepts, that can think some people have no right to be free.

Everybody owns themselves. It's all we've got. We have every right to be us. We have every right to satisfy our own needs with the life that we were given. I have no idea, no concept, of why people could ever think that they could own other people.

For My People

For my people everywhere singing their slave songs
repeatedly: their dirges and their ditties and their blues
and jubilees, praying their prayers nightly to an unknown
god, bending their knees humbly to an unseen power;

For my people lending their strength to the years, to the
gone years and the now years and the maybe years,
washing ironing cooking scrubbing sewing mending
hoeing plowing digging planting pruning patching
dragging along never gaining never reaping never
knowing and never understanding;

For my playmates in the clay and dust and sand of
Alabama backyards playing baptizing and preaching and
doctor and jail and soldier and school and mama and
cooking and playhouse and concert and store and hair
and Miss Choomby and company;

For the cramped bewildered years we went to school to
learn to know the reasons why and the answers to and the
people who and the places where and the days when, in
memory of the bitter hours when we discovered we were
black and poor and small and different and nobody cared
and nobody wondered and nobody understood;

For the boys and girls who grew in spite of these things to
be man and woman, to laugh and dance and sing and play
and drink their wine and religion and success, to marry
their playmates and bear children and then die of
consumption and anemia and lynching;

For my people thronging 47th Street in Chicago and
Lenox Avenue in New York and Rampart Street in New
Orleans, lost disinherited dispossessed and happy people
filling the cabarets and taverns and other people's pockets
needing bread and shoes and milk and land and money
and something—something all our own;

For my people walking blindly spreading joy, losing time
being lazy, sleeping when hungry, shouting when
burdened, drinking when hopeless, tied and shackled and
tangled among ourselves by the unseen creatures who
tower over us omnisciently and laugh;

For my people blundering and groping and floundering in
the dark of churches and schools and clubs and societies,
associations and councils and committees and
conventions, distressed and disturbed and deceived and
devoured by money-hungry glory-craving leeches, preyed
on by facile force of state and fad and novelty, by false
prophet and holy believer;

For my people standing staring trying to fashion a better
way from confusion, from hypocrisy and
misunderstanding, trying to fashion a world that will hold
all the people, all the faces, all the adams and eves and
their countless generations;

Let a new earth rise. Let another world be born. Let a bloody peace be written in the sky. Let a second generation full of courage issue forth; let a people loving freedom come to growth. Let a beauty full of healing and strength of final clenching be the pulsing in our spirits and our blood. Let the martial songs be written, let the dirges disappear. Let a race of men now rise and take control.

When I was attending Fisk—you are going to get tired of reading about my college memories—I used to like to hang around the library. I would have actually enjoyed working in the library, but there was no open work-study. I liked to be there because the library got all of the books, especially the new books. Fisk has a great collection of black literature, and all of the new books were there. Being an underclassman, I wasn't allowed to have a desk in the stacks. You had to be a graduate student to get one of those. A desk in the stacks meant that you had a place to go and read and nobody could bother you. It was your desk. You were allowed to do your research and your work. Still, I used to hang around in the library because I always did like libraries. I still like libraries.

I got to know people, and I started to do things that they didn't want to bother doing, and I offered free labor. I remember when *Jubilee* came in. I was just totally excited because I knew about Margaret Walker. I didn't know her personally. I knew her work, and I knew the poem *For My People*. When *Jubilee* came in I thought, "This is great, but I'm not letting anybody in this library stamp this book before I read it." I took it out and read it before it got officially in, and that way I had an opportunity to enjoy the book before anybody else had a chance to see it.

Margaret is one of my favorite people. I have done a book with her called *A Poetic Equation: Conversations Between Nikki*

Giovanni and Margaret Walker. Margaret has been overlooked
as the great intellect that she is. With *Jubilee* she was the first—
at least that I am aware of—to use the slaves' point of view in fiction. What she did, the ground she furrowed, Alex Haley visited
in *Roots,* and he won a Pulitzer Prize. And, of course Toni Morrison came along with *Beloved,* and in the meantime other people have begun to look at slavery. You have to give Margaret
credit for letting people know that this was possible; that if you
are a writer of fiction, you can do something from the slave point
of view; you don't always have to accept another point of view.

> *For my people everywhere singing their slave songs
> repeatedly: their dirges and their ditties and their
> blues and jubilees, praying their prayers nightly to
> an unknown god, bending their knees humbly to an
> unseen power;*

This is almost exactly a photograph of life in these United
States. She is simply looking at black people, at African Americans, and looking at the world as we see it. It is called a poem,
but it it also a prayer that in biblical times would be a lamenta-
tion: "Oh, Lord, hear my song; I love the Lord; He heard my
cry." She is describing the daily life of our people:

> *For my people lending their strength to the years, to the
> gone years and the now years and the maybe years,
> washing ironing cooking scrubbing sewing mending
> hoeing plowing digging planting pruning patching drag-
> ging along never gaining never reaping never knowing
> and never understanding;*

This is the story of Job, but Margaret, of course, didn't do it
that way, she didn't take that turn. She just simply shows: these
are my people. Then she gets more specific in the third stanza:

For my playmates in the clay and dust and sand of Alabama backyards playing baptizing and preaching and doctor and jail and soldier and school and mama and cooking and playhouse and concert and store and hair and Miss Choomby and company;

Margaret was born in Birmingham, Alabama, and grew up in Birmingham, so when she is speaking of that sand, she is not that far from the shore. We ended up calling Birmingham "Bombingham" because of so many bombings during the civil rights era, and she knows that.

For the cramped bewildered years we went to school to learn to know the reasons why and the answers to and the people who and the places where and the days when, in memory of the bitter hours when we discovered we were black and poor and small and different and nobody cared and nobody wondered and nobody understood;

For the boys and girls who grew in spite of these things to be man and woman, to laugh and dance and sing and play and drink their wine and religion and success, to marry their playmates and bear children and then die of consumption and anemia and lynching;

Consumption is tuberculosis, which was quite a big disease. We pretty much have conquered tuberculosis by this day and age, but with homelessness rising, tuberculosis is making a huge comeback in our major cities. Anemia we know, and she wasn't dealing with sickle cell, just the fact that people didn't have enough to eat. Then there is lynching. There is something especially poignant about the way that Margaret equates lynching with any other natural phenomenon that could be avoided. She lays out the cities:

*For my people thronging 47th Street in Chicago and
Lenox Avenue in New York and Rampart Street in New
Orleans, lost disinherited dispossessed and happy people
filling the cabarets and taverns and other people's pockets needing bread and shoes and milk and land and
money and something—something all our own;*

That is still the case. People will say to a welfare mother,
"Why don't you have money at the end of the month? Why
couldn't you save anything?" Take a situation where you are giving somebody 80 percent. You say the poverty level, the absolute
minimum that you need to live every month is $100, and then
someone decides "I'm only going to give you $80—and I expect
you to plan and budget, because, after all, you need to do that."
What kind of craziness is that? If somebody is at that level and
they need $100 simply to survive, it would make more sense to
give $150 so that they would have a little bit extra: a piece of
fruit, a little more ice cream, a glass of beer, anything that says
you are a human being and you, too, can enjoy the fruits of all of
our labor.

*For my people walking blindly spreading joy losing time
being lazy, sleeping when hungry, shouting when burdened, drinking when hopeless, tied and shackled and
tangled among ourselves by the unseen creatures who
tower over us omnisciently and laugh;*

She is saying so many white people look at so many of us as if
our lives were some sort of joke, as if our dreams and our aspirations had no truck, as if it shouldn't matter what we would like
for ourselves.

*For my people blundering and groping and floundering
in the dark of churches and schools and clubs and soci-*

eties, associations and councils and committees and con-
ventions, distressed and disturbed and deceived and de-
voured by money-hungry glory-craving leeches, preyed
on by facile force of state and fad and novelty, by false
prophet and holy believer;

She is doing some wonderful alliteration here when you get
that "distressed and disturbed and deceived and devoured."

For my people standing staring trying to fashion a better
way from confusion, from hypocrisy and misunderstand-
ings, trying to fashion a world that will hold all the
people, all the faces, all the adams and eves and their
countless generations;

Let a new earth rise. Let another world be born. Let a
bloody peace be written in the sky. Let a second genera-
tion full of courage issue forth; let a people loving free-
dom come to growth. Let a beauty full of healing and
strength of final clenching be the pulsing in our spirits
and our blood. Let the martial songs be written, let the
dirges disappear. Let a race of men now rise and take
control.

I'm sure, because Margaret is classically trained in her educa-
tion, that she was using "men" to mean all people. What she really meant was let a race of people, let a species rise and take
control. It's a wonderful poem because it is so imagistic. You actually can picture what she is saying. You see yourself. You see
the people that you know, and you know the hopelessness.
"Every good body ain't gone, but everybody's a-smiling and
laughin'."

Margaret is acknowledging that the life that we're living is
simply the best that we can do. When you are doing the best that

you can do, it is a damnable thing for someone else to laugh at you, for someone to put you down, for someone to say, "Why did you make this decision?"

People who have AIDS didn't make choices, they got a disease, they caught a disease. People who have cancer didn't make choices, they contracted a disease. And people who lost their jobs and lost their homes and people who had to file bankruptcy—these are not choices. Even if you were to say to yourself, "Well, goodness gracious, they didn't have to spend," or "They could have taken better care of themselves," you forget that nobody tries to court disaster. I suppose bungee jumpers and people like that might, but most of us are doing the best that we can do in the only way we know how, and sometimes we get lucky and it becomes all right. We catch ourselves before we fall, and sometimes we don't. That is being human.

It's good that Margaret says, "Let a new earth rise." Let a second generation loving freedom be born. It's important that somebody says, "Stop." It is like the story of the Tower of Babel: all these voices were going and finally the angel said, "Stop, you're disturbing the King." It's time that we all for a moment become quiet, to see what we can come up with, to see if we could find something else.

A Moment, Please

When I gaze at the sun
        I walked to the subway booth
        for change for a dollar
and know that this great earth
        Two adolescent girls stood there
        alive with eagerness to know
is but a fragment from it thrown
        all in their new found world
        there was for them to know.
in heat and flame a billion years ago,
        They looked at me and brightly asked
        "Are you Arabian?"
that then this world was lifeless
        I smiled and cautiously
          for one grows cautious—
        shook my head
as a billion hence,
        "Egyptian?"
it shall again be,
        Again I smiled and shook my head
        and walked away.
what moment is it that I am betrayed,
        I've gone but seven paces now
oppressed, cast down,
        and from behind comes swift the sneer
or warm with love or triumph?
        "Or Nigger?"

A moment, please
what is it that to fury I am roused?
   for still it takes a moment,
what meaning for me
   now
in this unrested clan
   . . . I turned
the dupe of space
   and smiled
the toy of time
   and shook my head.

Samuel Allen is a wonderful man. He is a courtly gentleman. I've had the pleasure of being able to read with him. Sam used to go by the name Paul Vesey. Denmark Vesey was the leader of a big slave rebellion in 1822 so it was a nice touch that he took on Vesey as part of his name. *A Moment, Please* is a poem that can be read two ways. You can read it only on the italics:

> *When I gaze at the sun*
> *and know that this great earth*
> *is but a fragment from it thrown*
> *in heat and flame a billion years ago,*
> *that then this world was lifeless*
> *as a billion hence,*
> *it shall again be,*
> *what moment is it that I am betrayed,*
> *oppressed, cast down,*
> *or warm with love or triumph?*
> *What is it that to fury I am roused?*
> *What meaning for me*

in this unrested clan
the dupe of space
the toy of time.

You can read it like that, and you have a fine poem. It lays out on the page. It is a demonstration of the duality that W. E. B. Du Bois talked about in *The Souls of Black Folk*. *A Moment, Please* is a trying to render into one body the inside and the outside.

At some point Sam could have said, "Yes, I'm Egyptian, definitely, now get the hell out of my way," or, "I'm Arabian." Sam Allen didn't look like any of those things. He looks like a black American. He is a medium-skinned guy with curly hair. He is a good-looking guy. The girls just wanted to play with him. These are the same little girls who, if they had been in Mississippi, would have gotten him lynched. And Sam just smiled and tried to go on his way.

View from the Corner

Now the thing the Negro has GOT to do—
     I looked from my uncle to my dad
Yes, Nimrod, but the trouble with the NEGRO is—
     I looked from my dad to my uncle
I know, Joseph, but the FIRST thing the Negro's got to
          do—
     It was confusing . . .

This fellow, the Negro, I thought excitedly,
     must be in a very bad fix—
We'd all have to jump in and help
     —such trouble

—all these things to do
I'd never HEARD of anybody with so many things to do
—GOT to do!
I intensely disliked such things
—go to school, wash your ears, wipe the dishes
And what the NEGRO had to do sounded worse than
    that!
He was certainly in a fix, this Negro, whoever he was.

I was much concerned as I looked at my uncle
Now the thing the Negro has GOT to do—!

In *View from the Corner* Sam is looking at current philosophy. It's funny because it's still the same thing. We are no longer called Negroes. Now we're African Americans, but the poem is still good. Everyone wants to make this situation of being black in America somehow a problem, and somehow, if it is going to be a problem, it is going to be a problem that the African American has to solve. That's ridiculous.

We didn't start it. We didn't start segregation. We didn't start lynching. We didn't start discriminating, and we are not going to be able to stop it. We can protest it, and we can make as many changes as we can, but somebody else is going to have to step in and say *this isn't right*. Because, clearly, if all black people had to do was to speak up, it would have stopped way before people like me were born. It would have stopped way before my mother was born. It would have stopped a long time ago if it was just up to us to stop it.

～ Gwendolyn Brooks (1917–)

Gwendolyn Brooks, the artist formerly known as Prince, and I share a birthday, though not at all in the same year. I remember reading Gwendolyn Brooks when I was in high school, maybe even junior high. I remember doing reports on her. I did a report on *Annie Allen*. I never thought when I was reading Miss Brooks that I would meet her. I knew she was alive, but writers are never really alive to people, and I was amazed when I was at a reading in Chicago and she came to it. It was just totally wonderful.

Gwen is a great human being, and she is very kind to young writers. We used to talk back and forth on the phone, because she mentored a lot of people. She didn't come to New York often, because she didn't fly, and I lived in New York. She still doesn't fly as far as I know. I do remember she was going to Africa, and she called because she was coming to New York. I said, "I would be really happy to take you out to dinner, where would you like to eat?" I think we ate at Benihana because she liked Japanese food. So when they came to New York with the people she was going with we went out and ate, and I said, "Gwen, I am just so surprised that you are going to Africa. I didn't realize they had completed the railroad line." She had to laugh. She said, "Okay, I'm going to fly, this one time I'm going to fly." I said, "Good for you," because I was happy she was going. You had to figure if you live in Chicago or New York you may as well fly for what can happen to you walking down city streets.

A Bronzeville Mother Loiters in Mississippi.
Meanwhile, a Mississippi Mother Burns Bacon.

From the first it had been like a
Ballad. It had the beat inevitable. It had the blood.
A wildness cut up, and tied in little bunches,
Like the four-line stanzas of the ballads she had never
      quite
Understood—the ballads they had set her to, in school.

Herself: the milk-white maid, the "maid mild"
Of the ballad. Pursued
By the Dark Villain. Rescued by the Fine Prince.
The Happiness-Ever-After.
That was worth anything.
It was good to be a "maid mild."
That made the breath go fast.

Her bacon burned. She
Hastened to hide it in the step-on can, and
Drew more strips from the meat case. The eggs
      and sour-milk biscuits
Did well. She set out a jar
Of her new quince preserve.

. . . But there was something about the matter of the
      Dark Villain.
He should have been older, perhaps.
The backing down of a villain was more fun to think
      about

When his menace possessed undisputed breadth,
      undisputed height,
And a harsh kind of vice.
And best of all, when his history was cluttered
With the bones of many eaten knights and princesses.

The fun was disturbed, then all but nullified
When the Dark Villain was a blackish child
Of fourteen, with eyes still too young to be dirty,
And a mouth too young to have lost every reminder
Of its infant softness.

That boy must have been surprised! For
These were grown-ups. Grown-ups were supposed to be
      wise.
And the Fine Prince—and that other—so tall, so broad, so
Grown! Perhaps the boy had never guessed
That the trouble with grown-ups was that under the
      magnificent shell of adulthood, just under,
Waited the baby full of tantrums.
It occurred to her that there may have been something
Ridiculous in the picture of the Fine Prince
Rushing (rich with breadth and height and
Mature solidness whose lack, in the Dark Villain, was
      impressing her,
Confronting her more and more as this first day after
      the trial
And acquittal wore on) rushing
With his heavy companion to hack down (unhorsed)
That little foe.   •

So much had happened, she could not remember now
    what that foe had done
Against her, or if anything had been done.
The one thing in the world that she did know and knew
With terrifying clarity was that her composition
Had disintegrated. That, although the pattern prevailed,
The breaks were everywhere. That she could think
Of no thread capable of the necessary
Sew-work.

She made the babies sit in their places at the table.
Then, before calling Him, she hurried
To the mirror with her comb and lipstick. It was necessary
To be more beautiful than ever.
The beautiful wife.
For sometimes she fancied he looked at her as though
Measuring her. As if he considered, Had she been
    worth It?
Had *she* been worth the blood, the cramped cries, the
    little stuttering bravado,
The gradual dulling of those Negro eyes,
The sudden, overwhelming *little-boyness* in that barn?
Whatever she might feel or half-feel, the lipstick necessity
    was something apart. He must never conclude
That she had not been worth it.

He sat down, the Fine Prince, and
Began buttering a biscuit. He looked at his hands.
He twisted in his chair, he scratched his nose.
He glanced again, almost secretly, at his hands.
More papers were in from the North, he mumbled. More
    meddling headlines.

With their pepper-words, "bestiality," and "barbarism,"
    and
"Shocking."
The half-sneers he had mastered for the trial worked
    across
His sweet and pretty face.

What he'd like to do, he explained, was kill them all.
The time lost. The unwanted fame.
Still, it had been fun to show those intruders
A thing or two. To show that snappy-eyed mother,
That sassy, Northern, brown-black—

Nothing could stop Mississippi.
He knew that. Big Fella
Knew that.
And, what was so good, Mississippi knew that.
Nothing and nothing could stop Mississippi.
They could send in their petitions, and scar
Their newspapers with bleeding headlines. Their
    governors
Could appeal to Washington . . .

"What I want," the older baby said, "is 'lasses on
    my jam."
Whereupon the younger baby
Picked up the molasses pitcher and threw
The molasses in his brother's face. Instantly
The Fine Prince leaned across the table and slapped
The small and smiling criminal.
She did not speak. When the Hand
Came down and away, and she could look at her child,

At her baby-child,
She could think only of blood.
Surely her baby's cheek
Had disappeared, and in its place, surely,
Hung a heaviness, a lengthening red, a red that had
     no end.
She shook her head. It was not true, of course.
It was not true at all. The
Child's face was as always, the
Color of the paste in her paste-jar.

She left the table, to the tune of the children's
     lamentations, which were shriller
Than ever. She
Looked out of a window. She said not a word. *That*
Was one of the new Somethings—
The fear,
Tying her as with iron.

Suddenly she felt his hands upon her. He had followed
     her
To the window. The children were whimpering now.
Such bits of tots. And she, their mother,
Could not protect them. She looked at her shoulders, still
Gripped in the claim of his hands. She tried, but could
     not resist the idea
That a red ooze was seeping, spreading darkly, thickly,
     slowly,
Over her white shoulders, her own shoulders,
And over all of Earth and Mars.

He whispered something to her, did the Fine Prince,
     something
About love, something about love and night and
     intention.
She heard no hoof-beat of the horse and saw no flash of
     the shining steel.

He pulled her face around to meet
His, and there it was, close close,
For the first time in all those days and nights.
His mouth, wet and red,
So very, very, very red,
Closed over hers.

Then a sickness heaved within her. The courtroom
     Coca-Cola,
The courtroom beer and hate and sweat and drone,
Pushed like a wall against her. She wanted to bear it.
But his mouth would not go away and neither would the
Decapitated exclamation points in that Other Woman's
     eyes.

She did not scream.
She stood there.
But a hatred for him burst into glorious flower,
And its perfume enclasped them—big,
Bigger than all magnolias.

The last bleak news of the ballad.
The rest of the rugged music.
The last quatrain.

The Last Quatrain of the Ballad of Emmett Till

> after the murder,
> after the burial
>
> Emmett's mother is a pretty-faced thing;
>   the tint of pulled taffy.
> She sits in a red room,
>   drinking black coffee.
> She kisses her killed boy.
>   And she is sorry.
> Chaos in windy grays
>   through a red prairie.

The Emmett Till case. I don't know if that's the proper term. It's not the Emmett Till case. Emmett Till was murdered. He was lynched.

The Till case was very, very hard on my generation because Emmett was just a boy. There had been a number of lynchings which we all knew about. We read *Jet*. We read the Chicago *Defender*. We read the Pittsburgh *Courier*. There were just always magazines in my home, and I spent summers with my grandmother, and my grandmother and grandfather were very politically active. There were other murders that we were aware of. There were other shootings. There were other bombings. There were other lynchings, and yet Till was just a boy. I think that was a part of the—you hate to say—shock because everybody should have known it was going on.

It had to come down to things like this. They lynched women. They lynched men. They did whatever their hatred led them to do. And yet to look at what happened to Emmett Till was a totally frightful thing.

The Till case was the first time that white men in the Deep South had been *charged* with the murder of a black person. It mattered. In the real world it mattered that they were going to free Roy Bryant and J. W. Milum. As the defense said, "I'm sure every Anglo-Saxon ounce of blood in you twelve men," and it was an all-white, all-male jury, "will free these men," and of course they did. It was no real surprise. Mrs. Bradley, Emmett Till's mother, was not surprised. Nobody was surprised. The surprise was that they were charged at all. For the first time the Klan had to go underground. The Klan is not still underground. The Klan has gone into the militia. The Klan now bombs federal buildings. It goes by any number of other names, but it is the same thing.

Gwendolyn Brooks's poem is brilliant. It is groundbreaking because it looked at the Till murder from the point of view of the person who reportedly was being protected. The poem is more or less from Caroline Bryant's point of view. How could Roy have done this in her name?

Gwen Brooks looked at the Till case and recognized that nobody could live with this burden. There is nobody on earth that was worth what that child went through, no matter what happened. In reality everybody knows that nothing happened. Absolutely nothing happened. Whatever he said, whatever he whistled, he did not do anything to Mrs. Bryant, and the price he paid for doing nothing was ridiculously high. The price the black community paid because we had to watch a child die, for what, for existing. That's crazy. So we have *A Bronzeville Mother Loiters in Mississippi.*

The sheriff asked Till's mother what was she doing in Mississippi. She said, "My son was killed." And he said, "What do you have to offer the trial?" She answered, "I know it's my boy." The sheriff was trying to say that the body they found was not really Till. "We are not even sure that it was a colored person. This is just a body, it has nothing to do with this case." It was so ridiculous. The sheriff wanted to say this boy, meaning Emmett Till, is probably up in Detroit having a good laugh at us. This is an embarrassment. That's so crazily sick you want to inject the antirabies serum just if you have to be around it.

> *From the first it had been like a*
> *Ballad. It had the beat inevitable. It had the blood.*
> *A wildness cut up, and tied in little bunches,*
> *Like the four-line stanzas of the ballads she had never*
>   *quite*
> *Understood—the ballads they had set her to, in school.*

> *Herself: the milk-white maid, the "maid mild"*
> *Of the ballad. Pursued*
> *By the Dark Villain. Rescued by the Fine Prince.*
> *The Happiness-Ever-After.*
> *That was worth anything.*
> *It was good to be a "maid mild."*
> *That made the breath go fast.*

> *Her bacon burned. She*
> *Hastened to hide it in the step-on can, and*
> *Drew more strips from the meat case. The eggs*
>   *and sour-milk biscuits*
> *Did well. She set out a jar*
> *Of her new quince preserve.*

> *. . . But there was something about the matter of the*
>   *Dark Villain.*
> *He should have been older, perhaps.*

The hacking down of a villain was more fun to think
  about
When his menace possessed undisputed breadth,
  undisputed height,
And a harsh kind of vice.
And best of all, when his history was cluttered
With the bones of many eaten knights and princesses.

Gwen is showing that this woman cannot live with the idea of the death of this child. How would you feel had this crime been committed in your name? You can't live with yourself. You either commit suicide, or, in the case of Caroline Bryant, I think she moved to Texas. You leave. And of course he's stuck there. He sold his story to *Life* magazine, to William Bradford Huey, and he claimed that, you know, he had to do it because white womanhood had to be protected. That's some kind of cruel joke. White womanhood could have said no.

Part of the Till case, too, was that one of Emmett's cousins asked Milum, "You just going to let that boy from Chicago get away with it?" as if it was some kind of test. I think his name was Mitchell Wright. I can't believe that Mitchell Wright thought that Emmett Till would be murdered, but it also says that when you start to play games with people's lives, people will lose their lives. When you play games, and lives are at stake, anything can go wrong.

In World War II they had all of those posters that warned "Loose lips sink ships." Half the time the sailors didn't know where they were going, because they didn't want them to tell their girlfriends. Otherwise their girlfriends might say, "Mack is going out to sea. He's going to be going toward the Indian Ocean," which could help the enemy. And yet a black boy in Mississippi, a young man challenged a white man, and said, "What are you going to do about what that boy from Chicago did?"

The boy from Chicago hadn't done anything. The boy from Chicago didn't have a clue that his life was in danger. At some point I'm sure he did, but as the events unfolded he did not. His granduncle, Mose Wright, had a clue. Mitchell, who died young, had a clue. Other people who heard the screams while Emmett was being beaten had a clue, but Emmett didn't have a clue. Emmett had no concept of what he had done to merit his life literally being beaten out of him.

I can't imagine the pain of somebody being beaten, literally beaten to death. I think the bullet in the side of his head is like the sword in the side of Jesus. It was a coup de grâce. He was being killed, if he wasn't already dead before they shot his head off.

You had Milum and Bryant totally crazy, but also caught up in a system that didn't allow for them to curb their insanity. Mitchell, or some young man, I think it was Mitchell, said, "What are you going to do about what that boy from Chicago did?" Instead of being able to say, "Nothing, the boy from Chicago didn't do anything," they had to assert themselves. They had to show that they were *the man,* that they were the important people.

Milum and Bryant tried to justify why they did that, tried to explain that it was about womanhood. It was about the purity of womanhood that made them viciously murder this child. That's just not believable. That's just not true. They murdered that child because they got caught up in their own hatred. It wasn't because of Caroline Bryant—or any other woman on the earth of any color, any race, any religion or creed—nobody needs to have that kind of crime committed in their name. It's unacceptable.

The Lovers of the Poor

arrive. The Ladies from the Ladies'
        Betterment League
Arrive in the afternoon, the late light slanting
In diluted gold bars across the boulevard brag
Of proud, seamed faces with mercy and murder hinting
Here, there, interrupting, all deep and debonair,
The pink paint on the innocence of fear;
Walk in a gingerly manner up the hall.
Cutting with knives served by their softest care,
Served by their love, so barbarously fair.
Whose mothers taught: You'd better not be cruel!
You had better not throw stones upon the wrens!
Herein they kiss and coddle and assault
Anew and dearly in the innocence
With which they baffle nature. Who are full,
Sleek, tender-clad, fit, fiftyish, a-glow, all
Sweetly abortive, hinting at fat fruit,
Judge it high time that fiftyish fingers felt
Beneath the lovelier planes of enterprise.
To resurrect. To moisten with milky chill.
To be a random hitching-post or plush.
To be, for wet eyes, random and handy hem.
        Their guild is giving money to the poor.
The worthy poor. The very very worthy
And beautiful poor. Perhaps just not too swarthy?
Perhaps just not too dirty nor too dim
Nor—passionate. In truth, what they could wish
Is—something less than derelict or dull.

Not staunch enough to stab, though, gaze for gaze!
God shield them sharply from the beggar-bold!
The noxious needy ones whose battle's bald
Nonetheless for being voiceless, hits one down.
            But it's all so bad! and entirely too much
            for them.
The stench; the urine, cabbage, and dead beans,
Dead porridges of assorted dusty grains,
The old smoke, *heavy* diapers, and, they're told,
Something called chitterlings. The darkness. Drawn
Darkness, or dirty light. The soil that stirs.
The soil that looks the soil of centuries.
And for that matter the *general* oldness. Old
Wood. Old marble. Old tile. Old old old.
Not homekind Oldness! Not Lake Forest, Glencoe.
Nothing is sturdy, nothing is majestic,
There is no quiet drama, no rubbed glaze, no
Unkillable infirmity of such
A tasteful turn as lately they have left,
Glencoe, Lake Forest, and to which their cars
Must presently restore them. When they're done
With dullards and distortions of this fistic
Patience of the poor and put-upon.
            They've never seen such a make-do-ness as
Newspaper rugs before! In this, this "flat,"
Their hostess is gathering up the oozed, the rich
Rugs of the morning (tattered! the bespattered. . . .)
Readies to spread clean rugs for afternoon.
Here is a scene for you. The Ladies look,
In horror, behind a substantial citizeness
Whose trains clank out across her swollen heart.

Who, arms akimbo, almost fills a door.
All tumbling children, quilts dragged to the floor
And tortured thereover, potato peelings, soft-
Eyed kitten, hunched-up, haggard, to-be-hurt.
          Their League is allotting largesse to the Lost.
But to put their clean, their pretty money, to put
Their money collected from delicate rose-fingers
Tipped with their hundred flawless rose-nails seems . . .
          They own Spode, Lowestoft, candelabra,
Mantels, and hostess gowns, and sunburst clocks,
Turtle soup, Chippendale, red satin "hangings,"
Aubussons and Hattie Carnegie. They Winter
In Palm Beach; cross the Water in June; attend,
When suitable, the nice Art Institute;
Buy the right books in the best bindings; saunter
On Michigan, Easter mornings, in sun or wind.
Oh Squalor! This sick four-story hulk, this fibre
With fissures everywhere! Why, what are bringings
Of loathe-love largesse? What shall peril hungers
So old old, what shall flatter the desolate?
Tin can, blocked fire escape and chitterling
And swaggering seeking youth and the puzzled wreckage
Of the middle passage, and urine and stale shames
And, again, the porridges of the underslung
And children children children. Heavens! That
Was a rat, surely, off there, in the shadows? Long
And long-tailed? Gray? The Ladies from the Ladies'
Betterment League agree it will be better
To achieve the outer air that rights and steadies,
To hie to a house that does not holler, to ring
Bells elsetime, better presently to cater

To no more Possibilities, to get
Away. Perhaps the money can be posted.
Perhaps they two may choose another Slum!
Some serious sooty half-unhappy home!—
Where loathe-love likelier may be invested.
            Keeping their scented bodies in the center
Of the hall as they walk down the hysterical hall,
They allow their lovely skirts to graze no wall,
Are off at what they manage of a canter,
And, resuming all the clues of what they were,
Try to avoid inhaling the laden air.

Riot

> A RIOT IS THE LANGUAGE OF THE UNHEARD.
>
> —MARTIN LUTHER KING, JR.

John Cabot—out of Wilma, once a Wycliffe
all whitebluerose below his golden hair,
wrapped richly in right linen and right wool,
almost forgot his Jaguar and Lake Bluff;
almost forgot Grandtully (which is the
Best Thing That Ever Happened To Scotch); almost
forgot the sculpture at the Richard Gray
and Distelheim; the kidney pie at Maxim's,
the *Grenadine de Boeuf* at Maison Henri.

Because the Negroes were coming down the street.   •

Because the Poor were sweaty and unpretty
(not like the Two Dainty Negroes in Winnetka)
and they were coming toward him in rough ranks.
In seas, in windsweep. They were black and loud.
And not detainable. And not discreet.

Gross. Gross. *"Que tu es grossier!"* John Cabot
itched instantly beneath the nourished white
that told his story of glory to the World.
"Don't let It touch me! the blackness! Lord!"
    he whispered
to any handy angel in the sky.

But, in a thrilling announcement, on It drove
and breathed on him: and touched him. In that breath
the fume of pig foot, chitterling and cheap chili,
malign, mocked John. And, in terrific touch, old
averted doubt jerked forward decently,
cried "Cabot! John! You are a desperate man,
and the desperate die expensively today."

John Cabot went down in the smoke and fire
and broken glass and blood, and he cried "Lord!
Forgive these nigguhs that know not what they do."

Gwendolyn Brooks has a wonderful view of rich people. These
people want to feel that they are doing good. They are philis-
tines. They want to feel that they are better than somebody, and
they have chosen the poor as long as the poor aren't too poor:

Their guild is giving money to the poor.
The worthy poor. The very very worthy
And beautiful poor. Perhaps just not too swarthy?
Perhaps just not too dirty nor too dim
Nor—passionate. In truth, what they could wish
Is—something less than derelict or dull.

What they want are the witty poor. They want the poor who are just sort of a bit out of favor, but not the arrogant poor, not the demanding poor. Gwen is not given much credit as a writer for her sense of humor, but when you read what she is doing here—and you know she has probably seen people like this—then you recognize that Ms. Brooks has a terrific sense of humor:

John Cabot—out of Wilma, once a Wycliffe
all whitebluerose below his golden hair,
wrapped richly in right linen and right wool,
almost forgot his Jaguar and Lake Bluff;
almost forgot Grandtully (which is the
Best Thing That Ever Happened To Scotch); almost
forgot the sculpture at the Richard Gray
and Distelheim; the kidney pie at Maxim's,
the Grenadine de Boeuf *at Maison Henri.*

Because the Negroes were coming down the street.

Because the Poor were sweaty and unpretty

Gwen has this white man who is so scared seeing the Negroes, he thinks he is going to drop dead. He doesn't know what to do with these Negroes walking down the street. This is a very, very funny point. But John Cabot, we know, is going to forget it all, because what he doesn't want to do is be bothered with the Negroes who are coming down the street.

Gwen brings one part of our story to an end. The people born in the late teens (she was born in 1917) begin to close out a certain way of looking at the world that opened with James Weldon Johnson. In a poem of hers called *The Preacher Ruminates Behind the Sermon,* she went back to the moment Johnson described in *The Creation.* He had shown a lonely God who set out to create a world. Gwen's God is different. He might sometimes tire "of being great / in solitude. Without a hand to hold." She does not imagine that God would build himself a partner or a friend. She sees that God is going to be all alone. That looks ahead to the next generation, the militants. Lance Jeffers, who was born in 1919, gives us yet another view of God. His God is one that we need.

On Listening to the Spirituals

When the master lived a king and I a starving hutted slave
    beneath
        the lash, and

when my five-year-old son was driven at dawn to
    cottonfield to pick
        until he could no longer see the sun, and

when master called my wife to the big house when
    mistress was gone,
took her against her will and gave her a dollar to be still,
    and
when she turned upon her pride and cleavered it, cursed
    her dignity
and stamped on it, came back to me with his evil on her
    thighs, hung
her head when I condemned her with my eyes,

what broken mettle of my soul wept steel, cracked teeth in
    self-contempt
upon my flesh, crept underground to seek new roots and
    secret breathing place?   •

When all the hatred of my bones was buried in a forgotten
    country of my soul,
then from beauty muscled from the degradation of my
    oaken bread,
I stroked on slavery soil the mighty colors of my song, a
    passionate
            heaven rose no God in heaven could create!

Lance is looking at why people created songs like "Sometimes I
Feel Like a Motherless Child." Why did people create songs
that voiced a longing to bury the hatreds?

It is very easy for Mr. Jeffers to see why we listen to the spirituals. We have to have something to carry us through that which
is unacceptable: your five-year-old son is required to be in the
cotton field; your wife is required to be in someone's bed; and
what about your daughter? We had to find a way to get through.
The old spiritual says, "His eye is on the sparrow, I know he's
watching me." The only answer had to be Jesus, some level of
God. We had to have the ability to raise a voice and to think that
someone is there to intercede. Not to save us from this pain, because nobody is crazy enough to ask to be spared the pain. What
you ask is the strength to be able to carry on despite it. That's
what the spirituals did, and that's what Lance Jeffers is responding to. "Lord, don't move the mountain, but give me the
strength to climb."

One of the fascinating aspects of the entire slavery experience
is that from 1619 essentially until freedom, black men did not
beat black women. Black men may have been upset, and probably were, about the fact that white men took black women, but
as Lance pointed out, against their will. If a male slave felt no
compassion for what his wife went through, he didn't beat her;
he didn't hit her, because she didn't belong to him, nor did she

belong to herself. It is an amazing thing that we come down to the last part of this century, the last blink, and now that we are supposed to be free, we go at each other. We beat each other; we abuse each other; we victimize each other. It is a ridiculous chain.

── LeRoi Jones / Amiri Baraka (1934–)

I met LeRoi Jones, although I'm sure he doesn't remember it, in 1963 I think it was, in Nashville, at Fisk actually. He was the major speaker at the Black Arts Festival. LeRoi (that was still his name at the time) wasn't a god to us but he wasn't far from it. I'm only nine years younger than LeRoi, but at that point it seemed that he was the big boy and we were the little kids just listening. He was the one to say, "Up against the wall motherfucker this is a stickup."

We had never heard anybody on a public stage say "motherfucker" before. It was electrifying. I really liked his possession of the language. LeRoi was a wonderful jazz poet. Since then he's been all over the map in terms of writing. He is actually a great American writer and perhaps even unfortunately for LeRoi he has gotten trapped in the period they call his nationalist period. He backed himself, he painted, if I were to use an imagistic term, he blacked himself into a corner. That was unfortunate because he is a wonderfully lyric poet.

The World Is Full of Remarkable Things

(FOR LITTLE BUMI)

Quick Night
easy warmth
The girlmother lies next to me
breathing
coughing
sighing

at my absence. Bird Plane
Flying near Mecca
Sun sight warm air
through
my air foils. Womanchild
turns
lays her head
on my stomach. Night aches
acts
Niggers rage

down the street. (Air
Pocket, sinks
us. She lady
angel brings
her self
to touch me
grains & grass & long
silences, the dark
ness my natural
element, in
warm black skin
I love &
understand
things. Sails
cries these
moans, pushed
from her by my
weight, her legs
spreading, wrapping
secure the spirit
in her.

        We begin our
ritual breathing
flex the soul clean
out, her eyes slide
into dreams

The World Is Full of Remarkable Things is just a beautiful poem. It is a lyric: "Quick Night / easy warmth / The girlmother lies next to me / breathing." This is a love poem. It's a poem that expresses some of his wonder, his awe at the world. We don't see that much of him. In the "Complete LeRoi Jones" or the "Complete Amiri Baraka" you would see this, but you don't see enough of it in his ordinary, everyday kind of poems.

I remember how LeRoi walked into the room, Jubilee Hall. He is a short man, and he had this mustache, but we had envisioned him as seven feet tall. So he kind of walks in, but he doesn't walk. He really charges in and he is very angry and the place was totally packed. It was not even SRO. It was beyond that. People were hanging on the windows outside to hear him, and he walked up onstage. We were screaming and shouting. He could have been a rock star as far as people like me were concerned because we were just screaming and shouting. We said, "LeRoi, LeRoi, LeRoi." He and James Baldwin have the most expressive eyes, and his eyes were just flashing and it was just like, "I am angry with the world." I thought, "Oh, great, it's really nice to be angry with the world."

It is difficult to be an artist, because what you can see needs to be done and what you can achieve are generally two very opposite things. The two are like yin and yang, north and south, positive and negative. What you see is just totally opposite of what the reality can be, and that's unfortunate. But there are things we can do. Writers can either repave—we fill in some of the cracks

in the road that are already there—or we start to knock down
some of the weeds to make a clearing in the wilderness. It is very
difficult, because you know that "If I could get everybody to
knock down these weeds with me then we would make this huge
change." We would be revolutionaries. But you have to content
yourself with the fact that "Oh, well, at least I brought a new
thought."

LeRoi would be an important American artist if he didn't do
anything but say "motherfucker," but he did a lot more than
that. He was the inspiration of an entire generation. Clearly people like me are going to have philosophical differences with people like LeRoi Jones because I like to do my own thinking. I
think that my understanding is sufficient unto my world, which
means that I am going to miss some things that other people see.
I'm also, though, not going to impose my views. It became very
sad to people like me when having a vision was not enough. Instead, some artists said that if you do not share this vision with
me, then we are going to ostracize you. You don't have to be
smart to ostracize people. People get ostracized all the time. But
what do you gain?

A Poem for Black Hearts

For Malcolm's eyes, when they broke
the face of some dumb white man. For
Malcolm's hands raised to bless us
all black and strong in his image
of ourselves, for Malcolm's words
fire darts, the victor's tireless
thrusts, words hung above the world
change as it may, he said it, and
for this he was killed, for saying,

and feeling, and being/change, all
collected hot in his heart, For Malcolm's
heart, raising us above our filthy cities,
for his stride, and his beat, and his address
to the grey monsters of the world, For Malcolm's
pleas for your dignity, black men, for your life,
black man, for the filling of your minds
with righteousness, For all of him dead and
gone and vanished from us, and all of him which
clings to our speech black god of our time.
For all of him, and all of yourself, look up,
black man, quit stuttering and shuffling, look up,
black man, quit whining and stooping, for all of him,
For Great Malcolm a prince of the earth,
let nothing in us rest
until we avenge ourselves for his death, stupid animals
that killed him, let us never breathe a pure breath if
we fail, and white men call us faggots till the end of
the earth.

A *Poem for Black Hearts* is about Malcolm, and we had heard a lot about Malcolm. I never did know Malcolm. I have had the privilege of meeting and working with Betty Shabazz, and I still consider and will always consider Betty Shabazz one of the great American women. I write about her a lot. I try to remember her in all of my poetry because she is a great woman.

Malcolm X was a great man with a wonderful sense of humor. Nobody with a smile like that could be anything but a loving man. I know a lot of white people who complain that Malcolm X did this, that, and the other. Malcolm meant exactly everything he said. It's become very fashionable to say now it was his

later period where he began to see that all colors could work together, that he really became important. I don't think so. He was
important when he said, "White people are devils." You can
look around at any day's headlines and tell me that these people
are not devils?

People say he hated. I don't think that's hate. Malcolm was
trying to say, "I'm upset; you people have disappointed me." If
he had been a godfather, he would have been Don Corleone. He
would have been able to sit there and say, "You disappoint me."
But, unless you are a godfather, nobody is going to listen to
somebody who is saying, "You disappoint me." So he said, "You
old blue-eyed thing," and everybody got mad. But he meant it at
the beginning and he meant it at the end. He meant it when he
said, "White people are a disappointment to planet Earth," and
he also meant it when he said, "We're going to have to find a way
to work together." There is no kind of sane logic that will allow
you to dismiss whole classes of people. Malcolm realized this, as
any thinking person must.

Malcolm had just been killed when we had the second arts
festival. He had been murdered. LeRoi said that everybody
should send poems for a book about Malcolm to Dudley Randall, who had started a press called Broadside in Detroit. Dudley
is a black man, a wonderful gentleman, and a poet. But I didn't
send a poem in. I didn't feel confident at that point to write
about Malcolm. I have subsequently done some things, but I
didn't feel like I should just knock off a poem, "Oh, brother
Malcolm, we're going to miss you so." The book did come out,
and it has a big X on it for Malcolm X. It's classic. It is a wonderful book, because I think almost everybody who was anybody—
and everybody that wasn't—contributed to it.

In *A Poem for Black Hearts* LeRoi was saying what we all believe, that Malcolm is our manhood. Malcolm is the guy who
stood up, and Malcolm is the guy who made the rest of us stand

up. Then, in a poem called *Black Art,* he wrote "poems are bull-shit unless they are teeth or trees or lemons piled on a step." It is so wonderful. It is so me. If I can say that it's wonderful and me, it's so *me* that you are going to make a poem trip some-body. *Black Art* is a strip-him-naked poem. If LeRoi could have made a poem a living thing, if he could have made the poem a bow, he would have put a word on an arrow and shot it into somebody's heart. He personified what the new black poetry was going to become, and he was uncompromising in that per-sonification.

Look for You Yesterday, Here You Come Today

Part of my charm:
    envious blues feeling
    separation of church & state
    grim calls from drunk debutantes

Morning never aids me in my quest.
I have to trim my beard in solitude.
I try to hum lines from "The Poet in New York."

People saw metal all around the house on Saturdays. The
                                  Phone rings.

terrible poems come in the mail. Descriptions of celibate
                    parties torn trousers: Great
                      Poets dying
                  with their strophes on. & me
                  incapable of a simple
                  straightforward anger.

It's so diffuse
being alive. Suddenly one is aware
   that nobody really gives a damn.
   My wife is pregnant with *her* child.
   "It means nothing to me," sez Strindberg

An avalanche of words
could cheer me up. Words from Great Sages.
     Was James Karolis a great sage??
     Why did I let Ora Matthews beat him
      up
     in the bathroom? Haven't I learned
     my lesson.
I would take up painting
if I cd think of a way to do it
better than Leonardo. Than Bosch.
Than Hogarth. Than Kline.

Frank walked off the stage, singing
"My silence is as important as Jack's incessant yatter."

I am a mean hungry sorehead.
Do I have the capacity for grace??
To arise one smoking spring
& find one's youth has taken off
for greener parts.

A sudden blankness in the day
as if there were no afternoon.
& all my piddling joys retreated
to their own dopey mythic worlds.

The hours of the atmosphere
grind their teeth like hags.

> (When will world war two be over?)

I stood up on a mailbox
waving my yellow tee-shirt
watching the grey tanks
stream up Central Avenue

> All these thots
> are Flowers Of Evil
> cold & lifeless
> as subway rails

the sun like a huge cobblestone
flaking its brown slow rays
primititi
> once, twice,. My life
> seems over & done with.
> Each morning I rise
> like a sleep walker
> & rot a little more.

All the lovely things I've known have disappeared.
I have all my pubic hair & am lonely.
There is probably no such place as Battle Creek,
    Michigan!

Tom Mix dead in a Boston Nightclub
before I realized what happened.   •

People laugh when I tell them about Dickie Dare!

What is one to do in an alien planet
where the people breath New Ports?
Where is my space helmet, I sent for it
3 lives ago . . . when there were box tops.

What has happened to box tops??

O, God . . . I must have a belt that glows green
in the dark. Where is my Captain Midnight decoder??
I can't understand what Superman is saying!

THERE *MUST* BE A LONE RANGER!!!

*****

but this also
is part of my charm.
A maudlin nostalgia
that comes on
like terrible thoughts about death.

How dumb to be sentimental about anything
To call it love
& cry pathetically
into the long black handkerchief
of the years.

> "Look for you yesterday
> Here you come today
> Your mouth wide open
> But what you got to say?"   •

   —part of my charm
     old envious blues feeling
     ticking like a big cobblestone clock.

I hear the reel running out . . .
the spectators are impatient for popcorn:
It was only a selected short subject

F. Scott Charon
will soon be glad-handing me
like a legionaire

My silver bullets all gone
My black mask trampled in the dust
& Tonto way off in the hills
moaning like Bessie Smith.

There is an old song, "Sent for You Yesterday." It's a blues song.
"Sent for you yesterday, and here you come today." Everybody
does that. That's like "a day late and a dollar short." It's all of the
old blues. Not the sad blues, more like Gene Ammons's happy
blues. Looked for you yesterday, and here you come today. It's a
rap; it is a strut; it is a very bold form. I like it a lot just because
it's fun. There must be a Lone Ranger, and yet the silver bullets are
gone, and this guy is looking for them. LeRoi is very funny, he can
be very funny; and that is one of the unknown parts of him. We
know him as an angry man, as a militant, we know him as a black
nationalist—as well we should—but he is also really quite funny.

   I hear the reel running out . . .
   the spectators are impatient for popcorn:
   It was only a selected short subject
   . . . .

My silver bullets all gone
My black mask trampled in the dust
& Tonto way off in the hills
moaning like Bessie Smith.

There must be a Lone Ranger. Hi-yo, Silver. This is a good read-aloud, and I like poems that lend themselves to that. We have to give ourselves over to the rhythm, to the intensity, to the fun of the poem.

personal letter no. 3

nothing will keep
us young you know
not young men or
women who spin
their youth on
cool playing sounds,
we are what we
are what we never
think we are.
no more wild geo
graphies of the
flesh, echoes, that
we move in tune
to slower smells.
it is a hard thing
to admit that
sometimes after midnight
i am tired
of it all.

One of my very favorite writers is Sonia Sanchez. She has a humorous side about her, and a sassy side, too. My favorite poem by Sonia Sanchez is *personal letter no. 3.*

Sonia probably has the best network in all the United States.

If you would catch—not a cold, say something a little more serious—say a tumor in your lung, Sonia would be on the phone to
Timbuktu, to California, to Florida. She must know every writer
on the face of this earth. She takes seriously her responsibilities
as "mother" to all of us. She is quite remarkable in her caring. It
is very nice to know that there is a community. It is easy to lose
track of community. But unless somebody puts community first,
community will be lost.

Sonia has made it a point of being available, of being there, of
passing the world a message, of letting people know what is
going on with their friends. That is not an easy thing to do. Yet it
is a necessity, and she takes the term "sister" very seriously. She
has done an extraordinary job in keeping up with all of us.

I chose this poem because it reflects something of Sonia
Sanchez that people don't necessarily think of when they think
of her firing off her mouth like a machine gun. You think of the
feisty way she goes at life. All of a sudden you have a poem that
says, "No, I think, I reflect upon things, I'm concerned about
some of it in another kind of way."

"Sometimes . . . I'm tired of it all." This connects to Dunbar,
to "we wear the mask." Dunbar is tired of it, too, and he says we
smile but we are smiling to hide this pain. Now, with Sonia, we
are coming full circle. Sonia is talking about our lives being ours,
and not allowing somebody else to come in and make a determi-
nation. There is that spiritual, "Will the Circle Be Unbroken?"
We hope that the circle will be broken, because we are coming
straight from Paul Laurence Dunbar to Sonia Sanchez, and we
are going to go a little bit farther than that, and we are going to
see that there is still this need, in Bob Hayden's words, this
"need to be free."

If one were to believe in reincarnation, Ishmael Reed is probably the reason that the slaves had their drums taken away from them. He is sarcastic. He was probably somewhere in the Middle Passage signifying on the white man, and somebody said, "Why does that boy have that drum? Take it away from him, don't let them Negroes have that drum." I'm sure it's all Ishmael's fault.

If you believe that human beings continue to evolve, you know that Ishmael Reed in the next three or four turnings of his soul will come out with hands that are drumsticks. His hands or his fingers will simply grow into those wonderful fan drumsticks jazz people use that just kind of tap along *che, che, che,* that really nice, calm, quiet sound. Yet there is a lot going on in jazz, so you can also hear the double rhythms. You can also hear the back beat on it. You can also hear him evolving all of these images, just raining down on you.

badman of the guest professor

FOR JOE OVERSTREET, DAVID HENDERSON,
ALBERT AYLER & D MYSTERIOUS "H"
WHO CUT UP D REMBRANDTS

1

you worry me whoever you are
i know you didn't want me to
come here but here i am just
d same; hi-jacking yr stagecoach,
hauling in yr pocket watches & mak
ing you hoof it all d way to

town. black bart, a robber w/ an
art; i left some curses in d cash
box so youll know its me

listen man, i cant help it if
yr thing is over, kaputs,
            finis
no matter how you slice it dick
you are done. a dead duck all out
of quacks; d nagging hiccupt dat
goes on & on w/ out a simple glass
            of water for relief

                              2
youve been teaching shakespeare for
20 years only to find d joke on you
d eavesdropping rascal who got it
in d shins because he didnt know
enough to keep his feet behind d cur
tains; a sad-sacked head served on a
platter in titus andronicus or falstaff
            too fat to make a go of it
            anymore

                              3
its not my fault dat yr tradition
was knocked off wop style & left in
d alley w/ pricks in its mouth. i
read abt it in d papers but it was no
            skin off my nose
wasnt me who opened d gates & allowed
d rustlers to slip thru unnoticed. you

ought to do something abt yr security or
        mend yr fences partner
dont look at me if all dese niggers
are ripping it up like deadwood dick;
doing art d way its never been done, mak
ing wurlitzer sorry he made d piano dat
will drive mozart to d tennis
        courts
making smith-corona feel like d red
faced university dat has just delivered china
        some 50 e-leben h bomb experts

i didnt deliver d blow dat drove d
abstract expressionists to mi ladies
linoleum where dey sleep beneath tons of
wax & dogshit & d muddy feet of children or
because some badassed blackpainter done sent
french impressionism to d walls of highrise
        lobbies where dey belong is not my fault
martha graham will never do d jerk
shes a sweet ol soul but her hips
cant roll; as stiff as d greek
statues she loves so much

                    4
dese are d reasons you did me nasty
j alfred prufrock, d trick you pull
ed in d bookstore today; stand in d
corner no peaches for a week, u lemon   •

u must blame me because yr wife is
ugly. 86-d by a thousand discriminating
saunas. dats why you did dat sneaky thing
i wont tell d townsfolk because u hv
to live here and im just passing thru

                         5
you got one thing right tho. i did say
dat everytime i read william faulkner i
go to sleep. when i read hemmingway i
wish dat one of dem bulls wd hv jumped d
fence & gored his fingers so dat he wdnt hv
taken up so much

                    good space

fitzgerald wdnt hv known a gangster if one
had snatched zelda & made her a moll tho
        she wd hv been grateful i bet

bonnie of clyde wrote d saga of suicide
sal just as d feds were closing in. it is
worth more than d collected works of ts
eliot a trembling anglican whose address
is now d hell dat thrilled him so
last word from down there he was open
ing a publishing co dat will bore d
devil back to paradise

6

& by d way did you hear abt grammar?
cut to ribbons in a photo finish by
stevie wonder, a blindboy who dances
on a heel. he just came out of d slang
& broke it down before millions.
            it was bloody murder

7

to make a long poem shorter—3 things
            moleheaded lame w/ 4 or 5 eyes
1) yr world is riding off into d sunset
2) d chips are down & nobody will chance yr i.o.u.s
3) d last wish was a fluke so now you hv to return to being
      a fish
p.s. d enchantment has worn off

dats why you didn't like my reading list   right?
it didn't include anyone on it dat you cd in
vite to a cocktail party & shoot a lot of
            bull   right?
so you want to take it out on my hide   right?
well i got news for you professor nothing—i
am my own brand while you must be d fantasy of
            a japanese cartoonist   •

a strangekind of dinosaurmouse
i can see it all now. d leaves
are running low. its d eve of
extinction & dere are no holes to
accept yr behind. you wander abt yr
long neck probing a tree. you think
its a tree but its really a trap. a
cry of victory goes up in d kitchen of
d world. a pest is dead. a prehis
toric pest at dat. really funnytime
prehistoric pest whom we will lug into
a museum to show everyone how really funny
you are   yr fate wd make a good
scenario but d plot is between you &
charles darwin. you know, whitefolkese
          business

as is said. im passing thru. just sing
ing my song. get along little doggie &
jazz like dat. word has it dat a big gold
shipment is coming to californy. i hv to
ride all night if im to meet my pardners
dey want me to help score d ambush

badman of the guest professor is fun, vicious in a way, but not vicious mean, because Ish is never vicious mean. But it is a vicious
kind of poem. It just puts everybody down. It puts down all of
Western civilization. It just puts down all the artists, and puts
them down very sweetly, very gently, very definitely, and then of
course does a dance over their graves.

Ish could not play professional football because they outlaw all kinds of celebration after touchdowns. That's silly. You score a touchdown, you really do want to stand in the end zone and go "Yaa," and show them that you're bad. Or in basketball, if you throw the ball down the hole, you slam dunk, you really are supposed to be able to show some kind of posture, but they don't want you to do that.

So people are going to come back to Ishmael Reed, and they're going to have to come back to poetry, and they are going to stand under the goalposts in football and recite a little bit: "its not my fault dat yr tradition / was knocked off wop style & left in / d alley." They'll do wonderful things like that, and everybody will say, "What is going on?" and pretty soon they'll outlaw poetry at football games, and it will all be the fault of Ishmael Reed. You will hear Ishmael in the NCAA final four and you will hear some NBA star slamming the ball down saying something smart that came straight, straight, straight out of Ishmael Reed's mouth.

✎— James Randall, Jr. (1938–   )

When Something Happens

Sometimes, when you're called a bastard
over a period, say,
of several centuries;
sometimes, when you've opened your brain
to a window in the sky,
become almost a bird for want
of flying;
sometimes, when a child walking
in your eyes is shot,
feeling, somehow, what you wish to forget,
through all cities your stark sorrow moving
where the sun leaks hideously
its garbage and the garbage
rots in your own stuffed room
and no one
in all the world gives a damn,
are firing rockets, are
ramming the roof of Heaven, are
crowning glory with glory . . .
Sometimes something happens   .

and happens and happens
when your breathing shape is tired to death
of being told
how well it lives,
how decent stinking ghetto,
the milk skimmed off to show, to demonstrate
this vegetable darkness.
When you are cheated, when
even netted fish find more freedom
and the eyes of stuffed beasts,
the eyes that never shut, seem
to mock you with their stuffed look—
you lead your blind family
from darkness to darkness,
on C Street on 5th Avenue look for work,
move your beast where
the white gods spit
and the El's grey slug sparks along tracks
and cattle are butchered far from farms
and farm boys wonder
who you are how so many millions
stand, shaded, different.   •

Let one word be spoken; let
the sky jump under your fists; let
the sun go out, drenched in your tears,
no leaf be still,
but the generations of trees transmuted
by your found anger; let
pushcarts lose their geometric rims,
the circles fall apart.
O God! Something
happens in this new world prison,
when prisoners rise up!

I think
the prairies are wildly waving.
I think
the zones are unbecoming.
I think
those divided cities are hovering in alliance;
in America, in America
as purified out of a final fire
you rise up, you continually elaborate
the tribal speech, the speech
of this Western tribe,
far from Africa, coming back, coming back
without the introvert bleating
about "origins."
You who will find your sleep
on a grass hill that is yours because you made it;
you, when the love has been worn out of you,
love still; on a flame hill,
the flame eating, give back a greater light,
who are, with the Indians,
the first Americans.

When *Something Happens* looks at the attack that the Western culture has made on people of color, but on black Americans specifically. It shows the way they tried to take away our Americanness from us, and yet these are the people who deliberately brought us here. It takes on the way they want to say this land was uninhabited, as it were, that Columbus "discovered" it. Columbus didn't discover America. He visited it, and saw that there were people there. People he took back to Europe.

James Randall looks at the reality of our lives:

> *Sometimes something happens*
>
> *and happens and happens*
> *when your breathing shape is tired to death*
> *of being told*
> *how well it lives,*
> *how decent stinking ghetto,*
> *the milk skimmed off to show, to demonstrate*
> *this vegetable darkness.*

We are still telling people how much better off they are: "Aren't you happy? Look at what we do for you." Randall is saying, "No, no, we can do a lot better than this, and I, Randall, am compelled to recognize that this is not the best of all possibilities, not the best of the possibilities that open up to me."

He and Ishmael go side by side, except of course that Ish is the trickster. Ish is a son of Shange, the Yoruba God of Thunder, and James Randall's poem is a quiet, reflective poem that says, "What my eyes see and what my heart feels could not be what my life is. I have to find a way around it. I have to find a way to do something just a little bit differently, to do something that makes a little more sense to me."

a poem (for langston hughes)

diamonds are mined . . . oil is discovered
gold is found . . . but thoughts are uncovered

wool is sheared . . . silk is spun
weaving is hard . . . but words are fun

highways span . . . bridges connect
country roads ramble . . . but i suspect

> if i took a rainbow ride
> i could be there by your side

metaphor has its point of view
allusion and illusion . . . too

meter . . . verse . . . classical . . . free
poems are what you do to me

let's look at this one more time
since i've put this rap to rhyme

> when i take my rainbow ride
> you'll be right there at my side

hey bop hey bop hey re re bop

USA *Today* called my office one day. It was a Tuesday, a pretty
day. I remember sitting there, the phone rang, I said, "Giovanni," because that's the way I answer the phone. A woman
said, "I'm from *USA Today* and we're going to do a feature on
poetry and we'd like to know if you could contribute to it." I
said, "Sure," thinking they want an interview or something of
that nature. The woman said, "We really would like a poem
from you." I said, "You'd like a poem from me?" Great. And
she said, "We'd like it on Wednesday or Thursday." I said,
"Wednesday and Thursday when?" "No, no," she said. "We
want it within two days." I said, "You're kidding."

But I thought about it and thought, "Okay, okay, I'm not
going to say I can't do it." So I said, "Well, okay, I'll do it. I'll
mail it over." And she said, "No, no, I want to give you the fax
number and you have to fax it over because we'll be just putting
it right in the paper and we need it at once. Not only by Thursday, but by Thursday at ten o'clock in the morning." The fax is
not your friend, because in the old days of the post office you
could always say, "Gee, I put it in the mail yesterday, I'm surprised you don't have it," one of those kind of things. But with a
fax, you fax it over at 9:00, it's supposed to be there at 9:05.

I was sitting in my office brooding. I have a small office. Actually I'm quite fortunate because at least it's mine, I don't have to
share it. It overlooks Virginia Tech; we have a drill field and my
office overlooks the drill field. I was just sitting, looking out my
window, pouting. I said to myself, and I think it's a human kind
of thing, "It isn't that *I* couldn't write a poem and have it there
overnight practically; nobody could." And then a little voice
said, "Langston Hughes could have done it."

It's true, Langston Hughes could have done it. I was still
pouting, but now it was okay, and I said, "If Langston Hughes
could have done it, what would he have done it on?" By now
I'm trying to think really, really hard. Langston said, "Always

write a love poem no matter what you're doing. Always write a love poem." That made sense. You should always love what you're doing. That's all he meant.

I thought, "Okay, I've got a subject because the subject is Langston Hughes, obviously, and it's going to be a love poem, love being love." Love's not all just pant, pant, pant. There are other aspects to love. Langston used to run those wonderful little couplets that were always so great. I never run couplets, but I thought, "This time I'm going to try to run couplets for Langston Hughes." So I wrote *a poem (for langston hughes)*. If you're going to do anything on poetry it ought to start, in all fairness, with Langston Hughes.

Nikki-Rosa

childhood remembrances are always a drag
if you're Black
you always remember things like living in Woodlawn
with no inside toilet
and if you become famous or something
they never talk about how happy you were to have
your mother
all to yourself and
how good the water felt when you got your bath
from one of those
big tubs that folk in chicago barbecue in
and somehow when you talk about home
it never gets across how much you
understood their feelings
as the whole family attended meetings about Hollydale
and even though you remember
your biographers never understand

your father's pain as he sells his stock
and another dream goes
And though you're poor it isn't poverty that
concerns you
and though they fought a lot
it isn't your father's drinking that makes any difference
but only that everybody is together and you
and your sister have happy birthdays and very good
Christmasses
and I really hope no white person ever has cause
to write about me
because they never understand
Black love is Black wealth and they'll
probably talk about my hard childhood
and never understand that
all the while I was quite happy

I looked at my childhood, as we all do. African Americans are great contemplators of our past, probably because we know so little about it. When I looked back, I began with what I knew to be a fact. We were poor, but it seemed to me that that was not the worst thing that happened to us. I am not recommending poverty, I never would. I am not like those people who sit around telling you it makes you a better person to want and need. It makes you crazy to want and need. But there are worse things in life than not having something.

I also know that no parent ever decided to be poor because you were coming. My parents didn't say, "Since we're expecting Nikki, why don't we sell the stocks and bonds?" It doesn't happen that way. We were poor because we were poor. We were poor before I came along, and we were going to be poor after I

came along, and it had nothing to do with me. I've never understood that about rich or poor people. People are ashamed of
being poor and people are very proud of being rich, and the reality is that we don't have anything to do with it. We happen to
be born, and we happen to have survived.

Your childhood was good because you survived it, whatever
else, no matter what condition you're in, you've survived it. Nobody really remembers childhood. I'm always amazed that people will say things like, "You were a terrible child, you cried all
the time," stupid things like that. One thing is for sure, you
don't remember that you were up all night. People actually say
things like, "Lord, I thought you were going to kill your mother
when you were being born." What is wrong with these people?
You didn't do anything. You were trying to be born. You didn't
have anything to do with it.

I liked my childhood, and I think that it was good. It is sane to
like your childhood, because if you don't, you spend all of your
life being unhappy about something that's not going to change
anyway. No matter what you do. Childhood is not a question of
what it was; it's a question of how you interpret it. And it seemed
to me that it was a good thing. We had a good neighborhood.
We had friends. We had things to eat and things to do and
grown-ups to snoop around on. It was life and it was good. It
was neither exceptional nor unexceptional.

We did the best we could, and I think most people do the best
that they can. I wanted to write a poem, because I really just got
sick of everybody making something else out of it. It's just the
life you're trying to live.

— Carolyn M. Rodgers (1945–)

It Is Deep

(don't never forget the bridge
that you crossed over on)

Having tried to use the
witch cord
that erases the stretch of
thirty-three blocks
and tuning in the voice which
   woodenly stated that the
   talk box was "disconnected"

My mother, religiously girdled in
her god, slipped on some love, and
laid on my bell like a truck,
blew through my door warm wind from the south
concern making her gruff and tight-lipped
    and scared
that her "baby" was starving.
she, having learned, that disconnection results from
    non-payment of bill(s).   •

She did not
recognize the poster of the
grand le-roi (al) cat on the wall
had never even seen the books of
Black poems that I have written
thinks that I am under the influence of
           communists
when I talk about Black as anything
other than something ugly to kill it befo it grows
     in any impression she would not be
considered "relevant" or "Black"
                                        but
there she was, standing in my room
not loudly condemning that day and
not remembering that I grew hearing her
curse the factory where she "cut uh slave"
and the cheap j-boss wouldn't allow a union,
not remembering that I heard the tears when
they told her a high school diploma was not enough,
and here now, not able to understand, what she had
been forced to deny, still—

she pushed into my kitchen so
she could open my refrigerator to see
what I had to eat, and pressed fifty
bills in my hand saying "pay the talk bill and buy
some food; you got folks who care about you . . ."

My mother, religious-negro, proud of
having waded through a storm, is very obviously,
a sturdy Black bridge that I
crossed over, on.

Carolyn Rodgers looks at her family, too. She says "don't never forget that bridge that you crossed over on." This is a fine poem about her mother. Her mother, like all mothers, worried about her. Her mother called and the phone had been disconnected, because Carolyn didn't have any money, so her mother did what anybody else would do. She got dressed and went over to see about her baby. All of this militant talk, all of this talk about who she was or who she wanted to be, her mother wanted to know, "Are you all right?" And her mother just wanted to say, "I cut a slave," which is another word for a job. "I worked. I took care of myself. I took care of you." This is quite poignant, because we thought we were so wonderful and so revolutionary and we thought we had so many new concepts that nobody ever heard of. We as a generation had to sit down and think it through for a minute, and we finally realized everybody has felt the same thing.

it's not so good to be born a girl / sometimes.

that's why societies usedta throw us away/ or sell us/ or
play with our vaginas/ cuz that's all girls were good for. at
least women cd carry things & cook/ but to be born a girl
is not good sometimes/ some places/ such abominable
things cd happen to us. i wish it waz gd to be born a girl
everywhere/ then i wd know for sure that no one wd be
infibulated/ that's a word no one wants us to know.
infibulation is sewing our vaginas up with cat-gut or
weeds or nylon thread to insure our virginity. virginity
insurance equals infibulation. that can also make it
impossible for us to live thru labor/ make it impossible for
the baby to live thru labor. infibulation lets us get
infections that we cant mention/ cuz disease in the ovaries
is a sign that we're dirty anyway/ so wash yrself/ cuz once
infibulated we have to be cut open to have/ you know
what/ the joy of the phallus/ that we may know nothing
about/ ever/ especially if something else not good that
happens to little girls happens: if we've been excised. had
out labia removed with glass or scissors. if we've lost our
clitoris because our pleasure is profane & the presence of
our naturally evolved clitoris wd disrupt the very
unnatural dynamic of polygamy. so with no clitoris/ no
labia & infibulation/ we're sewn-up/ cut-up/ pared down
& sore if not dead/ & oozing pus/ if not terrified that so
much of our body waz wrong & did not belong on earth.
such thoughts lead to a silence/ that hangs behind veils &

straightjackets/ it really is not so good to be born a girl
when we have to be infibulated, excised, clitorectomized
& STILL be afraid to walk the streets or stay home at
night. i'm so saddened that being born a girl makes it
dangerous to attend midnight mass unescorted. some
places if we're born girls & someone else who's very sick
& weak & cruel/ attacks us & breaks our hymen/ we have
to be killed/ sent away from our families/ forbidden to
touch our children. these strange people who wound little
girls are known as attackers/ molesters & rapists. they are
known all over the world & are proliferating at a rapid
rate. to be born a girl who will always have to worry not
only abt the molesters/ the attackers & the rapists/ but
also abt their peculiarities: does he stab too/ or shoot?
does he carry an axe? does he spit on you? does he know
if he doesnt drop sperm we cant prove we've been
violated? these subtleties make being a girl too complex/
for some of us & we go crazy/ or never go anyplace. some
of us have never had an open window or a walk alone, but
sometimes our homes are not safe for us either. rapists &
attackers & molesters are not strangers to everyone/ they
are related to somebody/ & some of them like raping &
molesting their family members better than a girl-child
they don't know yet. this is called incest, & girl children
are discouraged from revealing attacks from uncle or
daddy/ cuz what wd mommy do? after all/ daddy may
have seen to it that abortions were outlawed in his state/
so that mommy might have too many children to care abt
some "fun" daddy might be having with the 2-yr-old/
she's a girl after all/ we have to get used to it. but
infibulation, excision, clitorectomies, rape & incest are
irrevocable life-deniers/ life stranglers & disrespectful of

natural elements. i wish these things wdnt happen anywhere anymore/ then i cd say it waz gd to be born a girl everywhere. even though gender is not destiny/ right now being born a girl is to be born threatened; i want being born a girl to be a cause for celebration/ cause for protection & nourishment of our birthright/ to live freely with passion/ knowing no fear that our species waz somehow incorrect. & we are now plagued with rapists & clitorectomies. we pay for being born girls/ but we owe no one anything/ not our labia, not our clitoris, not our lives. we are born girls to live to be women who live our own lives/ to live our lives. to have/ our lives/ to live. we are born girls/ to live to be women . . .

Ntozake Shange tells us *it's not so good to be born a girl.* She does not object to being born a girl. She objects to what it means when you are born a girl. She objects to the way that girls are treated. She objects to the way that our dreams are stifled. She objects to the way that we are not taken seriously, we are there as some sort of plaything.

W. E. B. Du Bois started this book saying, "I am the smoke king, I am black." I am the energy, I am the fuel that lights this fire. Ntozake ends us with "it's not so good to be born a girl/ sometimes." It's amazing to me that the same point of view—of being denied because we are black—can come down to one of the youngest poets in the continuing saga of the Harlem Renaissance. She changes the gender, but she shows that it's still difficult to be born black.

And yet I know that the world changes. I know that life does not go around in circles. Life goes in cycles, so there's a continual spiral and we're always reaching for a better definition of a human being. You can always find a villain. Emmett Till teaches us that. You can always find a villain, a fourteen-year-old villain. You can always find a villain, a blue-eyed devil. You can always find a villain, a man, a woman. You can always find a villain, a child. You can always find a reason. But the reality is we're just still struggling, all of us, to stay alive. The reality is we're hoping that there is a God someplace who indeed does keep his eye on the sparrow, and we do indeed hope he watches us, and that somehow the mystery and the majesty of the unknown will inform our curiosity as well as our furies. The Renaissance teaches us this, too.

What you really hate is the people who are dream snatchers. You hate the people that say things like "There's no tooth fairy." I know there's a tooth fairy. I find pennies all the time, and I don't have a tooth. I know that there's a tooth fairy. And I know that there's a Santa Claus. I know that there's an Easter bunny, because there are always colored eggs all around.

I just resent the people who refuse to accept the responsibility for being human, and a part of that responsibility is to recognize the mystery, and try to understand the majesty, and that's all that we are doing here on this planet.

The Renaissance, the rebirth of Harlem, the recognition of that flame involved laughter, and music, and even a dress. The chemise is such a simple dress; it's actually a peasant dress, a slave dress. When you think about the chemise, you're thinking about what is basically a flour sack. It was a flour sack that just barely covers the hips and buttocks of some woman who decided, well—what did Julian Bond say—"Look at that gal shake that thing. We can't all be Martin Luther King."

I'm sure back in the 1900s, as this country is getting ready to go fight in the First World War, as people are migrating to the north, you have these sacks and they are hugging the hips and somebody said, "I know, I can't do a lot of things. I can't write books. I can't write poems. Maybe I can't paint. I don't sculpt. I'm not sure what my talents are, but, hey, I can shimmy, shimmy, shimmy. I can move my hips from side to side."

I think that we're lucky that we're still living with the influence of a people who believed that if we could write a poem, if we could sing a song—I suppose if we were looking at it today, if we could make a rap—if we could find a way to tell people that we, too, have dreams, they would honor our humanness. I think that's a great calling. I think it's something we need to be very proud of.

⚡ Biographical Notes

SAMUEL ALLEN (1917–   ). Descended from a highly literary and socially active family—Allen's paternal grandfather was editor of the *Southern Christian Recorder,* his maternal grandmother was Booker T. Washington's secretary and a poet in her own right, and his mother was "class poetess" at Clark College—Samuel Allen was heavily influenced by the Harlem Renaissance. A member of James Weldon Johnson's creative writing workshop at Fisk University, a graduate of Harvard Law School, and a professor first at Tuskegee Institute then later at Boston University, Allen has had a distinguished career as both a legal and literary scholar. Some of his published works include *Ivory Tusks and Other Poems* (1968), his 1971 essay "The African Heritage," and *Paul Vesey's Ledger* (1975), a collection of poetry.

AMIRI BARAKA (LEROI JONES UNTIL 1968) (1934–   ). Reared in Newark, New Jersey, Amiri Baraka spent his early days as a poet in New York City's Greenwich Village with Beat poets like Allen Ginsberg and Diane di Prima. His first published volume of poetry, *Preface to a Twenty Volume Suicide Note* (1961), reflects this Beat influence. By 1963 Baraka had embraced a growing black nationalist movement. *Blues People* (1963), his two-scene play *Dutchman* (1964), and the non-fiction collection *Home: Social Essays* (1965), reflect this change. Amiri Baraka continues to write poetry. Some of his more recent works include *The Autobiography of LeRoi Jones/Amiri Baraka* (1984), *Shy's, Wise, Y's: The Griot's Tale* (1994), *Jesse Jackson and Black People* (1994), and *Transbluesency: The Selected Poems of Amiri Baraka (LeRoi Jones)* (1995).

ARNA BONTEMPS (1902–1973). The son of a stonemason father and schoolteacher mother, Arna Bontemps grew up in California, where he attended Pacific Union College. Upon graduating in 1924, Bontemps, who had been submitting poetry to the *Crisis,* moved to Harlem, where he began a lifelong friendship with Langston Hughes. In 1926 Bontemps's *Golgotha Is a Mountain* won *Opportunity*'s Alexander Pushkin Award for Poetry, and, in 1927, the *Crisis*'s first prize for poetry. His first novel, *God Sends Sunday,* was published in 1931. Bontemps went on to the post of head librarian at Fisk University. Some of his other works include *Black Thunder* (1935), *Drums at Dusk* (1939), and an anthology, *The Poetry of the Negro, 1746–1949,* which he collaborated on with Langston Hughes.

GwendolyN Brooks (1917–   ). Gwendolyn Brooks was born in Topeka, Kansas, but has lived most of her life in Chicago. Her first collection of poetry, *A Street in Bronzeville,* was published in 1945. Five years later she won a Pulitzer Prize for *Annie Allen* (1949), the first awarded to an African American for a poetry collection. The recipient of numerous awards and honors, including two Guggenheim Fellowships (1946, 1947), she continues to write poetry.

CounteE CulleN (1903–1946). Adopted at the age of fifteen by the Rev. Frederick Asbury Cullen, one of Harlem's leading ministers, Countee Cullen was a precocious youth who became a leading Harlem Renaissance poet. He graduated Phi Beta Kappa from New York University and was a recipient of the Witter Bynner Poetry Prize in 1925. Cullen's first collection of poetry, *Color,* was published that same year to much critical acclaim. In 1926 he obtained a master's degree from Harvard, and in 1928 was awarded a Guggenheim Fellowship—the first African American to receive this prestigious honor. By the end of the twenties, Cullen had produced *Copper Sun* and the *Ballad of a Brown Girl,* as well as two poetry anthologies, *Caroling Dusk* and *The Black Christ and Other Poems.* From 1934 until the end of his life, Countee Cullen taught in New York City public schools.

WariNq CuNEy (1906–1976). Best known for his poem *No Images,* which won first prize out of 1,276 entries in the *Opportunity* poetry contest of 1926. Cuney's poetry was often published in anthologies, such as Countee Cullen's *Caroling Dusk* (1927), and in magazines like

Fire!!! Although he was not as prolific as some of the other Renaissance poets, he continued to write until his death in 1975.

William Edward Burghardt Du Bois (1868–1963). Writer, poet, sociologist, political activist, and scholar, Du Bois is considered one of the most important African-American leaders of the twentieth century. Born and reared in Great Barrington, Massachusetts, he graduated with honors from Fisk University in 1888, then received his Ph.D. in American history from Harvard. Du Bois was also a devoted sociologist. In 1899 he published the first case study of a black community in the United States, entitled *The Philadelphia Negro: A Social Study.* Du Bois gradually came to believe that, in a racially charged culture, social change could only be accomplished through protest, a view that contrasted sharply with that of Booker T. Washington, who urged blacks to accept discrimination and better themselves through hard work and economic gain.

His seminal work, *The Souls of Black Folk,* was published in 1903, and in 1905 Du Bois founded the Niagara Movement, forerunner to the National Association for the Advancement of Colored People (NAACP). In 1909 he played a prominent role in the creation of the NAACP, and he served as the association's director of research and editor of its magazine, *Crisis.* Some of his other published works include *The Quest for the Silver Fleece* (1912) and *The Dark Princess* (1928). In 1961, after joining the Communist Party and renouncing his American citizenship, Du Bois moved to Ghana, where he died in 1963.

Paul Laurence Dunbar (1872–1906). Paul Laurence Dunbar was the first African-American writer to gain national prominence. Born in Dayton, Ohio, to parents who had been slaves, Dunbar attended an all-white high school, where he became the editor of the school paper. He published his first volume of poetry, *Oak and Ivy,* in 1893 at his own expense while working as an elevator operator, selling copies to passengers to pay for the printing. His second volume of poetry, *Majors and Minors,* was published in 1896 and received a strong reception. Dunbar wrote both fiction and verse, publishing four collections of short stories and four novels before an early death in 1906, brought on by tuberculosis and alcohol.

MARCUS GARVEY (1887–1940). Social activist, political organizer, and entrepreneur, Marcus Garvey, or "Black Moses" as he was called by his followers, organized the first major black nationalist movement in Harlem. Born in St. Ann's Bay, Jamaica, and reared by fiercely proud African parents, Garvey left in 1907 to pursue job interests in Central America and then England. Upon returning to Jamaica in 1914, he founded the Universal Negro Improvement and Conservation Association and African Communities League (later shortened to UNIA). Garvey arrived in Harlem in 1919 and created *The Negro World,* a newspaper that was printed in English, Spanish, and French. It spoke of a "new Negro," who was proud to be black. Garvey believed that African Americans would be respected only when they were economically strong, and he fought for an independent black economy within the framework of white capitalism. Indicted for mail fraud in 1922, Garvey was dubbed an undesirable alien and deported by the U.S. government. He died in obscurity in London in 1940.

Nikki Giovanni (1943–   ). Poet, recording artist, writer, scholar, teacher, political and social activist, Nikki Giovanni has published more than twenty books in a career that spans three decades. In addition to eight honorary doctorate degrees, she has been awarded *Mademoiselle* magazine's prestigious Woman of the Year Award (1971) and the Ohioana Book Prize for *Sacred Cows . . . and Other Edibles* (1988). Some of her published works include *Spin a Soft Black Song* (1971), *Ego Tripping and Other Poems for Young Readers* (1973), *Knoxville, Tennessee* (1994), *Racism 101* (1994), and *Grand Mothers: Poems, Reminiscences, and Short Stories About the Keepers of Our Traditions* (1994). Nikki Giovanni is a professor of English at Virginia Polytechnic Institute in Blacksburg, Virginia.

Robert Hayden (1913–1980). Born and reared in Detroit, Robert Hayden graduated from Detroit City College (now Wayne State University) in 1936. After completing his first book of poetry, entitled *Heart-Shape in the Dust* (1940), he enrolled in a master's program at the University of Michigan, where he studied with and was befriended by W. H. Auden. In 1946 Hayden accepted a position at Fisk University, remaining there for twenty-two years. During this period, he wrote

The Lion and the Archer (1948), *Figure of Time* (1955), *A Ballad of Remembrance* (1962)—for which he won the Grand Prize for Poetry in English at the First World Festival of Negro Arts—and *Selected Poems* (1966). In 1975 Hayden was elected a fellow of the American Academy of Poets, and in 1976 he became the first African American to be appointed poetry consultant to the Library of Congress. Hayden taught at the University of Michigan at Ann Arbor until his death in 1980.

LANGSTON HUGHES (1902–1967). Possibly the most significant black American writer of the twentieth century, Langston Hughes has authored poems, novels, short stories, dramas, and translations that span from the early days of the Harlem Renaissance to the black arts movement in the late 1960s. Reared by his grandmother and mother, Hughes attended high school in Cleveland, Ohio. One year after graduating, he gained considerable attention when his poem *The Negro Speaks of Rivers* was published in the *Crisis* in 1921. After a brief stint at Columbia, then a trip to West Africa and Europe, Hughes returned to the United States, where, while working as a busboy at a hotel in Washington D.C., he is said to have been "discovered" by the poet Vachel Lindsay. Two books followed, *The Weary Blues* (1926) and *Fine Clothes to the Jew* (1927). In 1929 he received his undergraduate degree from Lincoln University. Langston Hughes went on to publish many books of poetry and prose, including *Not Without Laughter* (1930), *The Ways of White Folks* (1934), and his autobiography, *The Big Sea* (1940), which covers his life up to the age of twenty-eight.

LANCE JEFFERS (1919–1985). While Lance Jeffers's poetry began appearing in anthologies in 1962, his 1970 collection, *My Blackness Is the Beauty of This Land,* established him as an important literary voice. In 1974 Jeffers became a professor of English at North Carolina State University, and he went on to publish other poetry collections, including *O Africa, Where I Baked My Bread* (1977) and *Grandshire* (1979).

HELENE JOHNSON (1907–1995). One of the youngest and brightest poets of the Harlem Renaissance, Helene Johnson arrived in New York from Boston with her cousin, Dorothy West, just as the Renaissance was getting under way. Her award-winning poems include *My*

Race and *Metamorphism,* published in the March 1926 issue of *Opportunity,* and *Bottled,* published in *Vanity Fair* in May 1927. She suddenly and somewhat mysteriously disappeared from the New York literary scene in 1929. A 1988 article revealed that Johnson had left New York to dedicate herself to raising her daughter and earning a livelihood.

JAMES WELDON JOHNSON (1871–1938). After receiving his undergraduate and master's degrees from Atlanta University, James Weldon Johnson returned to his home in Florida, where he headed a grammar school, founded a newspaper, the *Daily American,* and passed the Florida bar exam, becoming the first black lawyer in Florida. Amazingly, he found the spare time to write and compose music. In 1901 he and his brother traveled to New York City, where they wrote over two hundred songs for the New York stage.

In 1906 President Theodore Roosevelt appointed Johnson U.S. consul to Venezuela, and in 1909 consul to Nicaragua, where he served until 1912. Being abroad gave Johnson the time to pursue his writing interests. In 1912, his *Autobiography of an Ex-Colored Man* was published, and then in 1917 his widely acclaimed *Fifty Years and Other Poems.*

In 1918, at the request of W. E. B. Du Bois, Johnson became a field organizer for the NAACP. His 1922 *The Book of American Negro Poetry, with an Essay on the Negro's Creative Genius* was well received, as was *Black Manhattan* (1930), the first history of the African American in New York. Returning to Fisk University after a vacation in New England with his wife in 1938, James Weldon Johnson died when their car crashed into a train.

CLAUDE MCKAY (1890–1948). Born in rural Jamaica, McKay traveled to Tuskegee Institute in Alabama to study agriculture. However, it was poetry that interested him. After transferring and then graduating from Kansas State College in 1917, McKay arrived in Greenwich Village, New York, intent on being a part of the growing bohemian scene. However, McKay quickly became disenchanted with race relations in America. He left for Russia in 1922, living in many different countries before he returned to New York in 1934. Some of his better-known works include *Harlem Shadows: The Poems of Claude McKay* (1922), *Home to Harlem* (1928), and his autobiography, *A Long Way from Home* (1937).

JAMES A. RANDALL (1938–   ) has produced two books of poems, *Don't Ask Me Who I Am* and *Cities and Other Disasters.* His poetry has appeared in several anthologies and has been translated into Dutch and Hebrew.

ISHMAEL REED (1938–   ). The author of eight novels—including *Mumbo Jumbo* (1973), *Yellow Back Radio Broke-Down* (1975), and *The Last Days of Louisiana Red* (1989)—four books of poems, two collections of essays, and the editor and publisher of several anthologies, Ishmael Reed is one of the more prominent figures in African-American literature today. He has taught at Berkeley, Yale, Dartmouth, Harvard, and, more recently, the University of California, Santa Barbara. Ishmael Reed lives with his wife and daughter in the San Francisco area.

CAROLYN M. RODGERS (1945–   ). Well known since the mid-seventies for her poetry about the role of the black woman in a changing society, Carolyn M. Rodgers emerged from the Chicago Organization of Black American Culture Writers' Workshop during the 1960s. Her first major collection of poetry, entitled *Paper Soul,* was published in 1968 and won her the Conrad Kent Rivers Memorial Fund Award. In 1969 her *Songs of a Blackbird* appeared, and then in 1975 *how i got ovah: New and Selected Poems.* A music lover, Rodgers continues to write and teach.

SONIA SANCHEZ (1935–   ). While her sixties poetry often reflected her strong militant outlook, Sonia Sanchez has become many things in addition to a socially active poet: teacher, playwright, editor, children's book author, and scholar. She is well known for her use of traditional chants and near-screams at readings. Some of her published works include *We a BaddDDD People* (1970), *A Blues Book for Blue Black Magical Women* (1973), *I've Been a Woman* (1981), and *Under a Soprano Sky* (1987). Sanchez has taught at many different institutions, including Rutgers, Amherst, the University of Pennsylvania, and, more recently, Temple University. She continues to write and teach.

NTOZAKE SHANGE (1948–). Ntozake Shange exploded into the book and theater world in the mid-seventies with her production of *for colored girls who have considered suicide/when the rainbow is enuf* (1976), which won the 1977 Obie, Outer Critics Circle, and *Mademoiselle* awards, and received Tony, Grammy, and Emmy nominations. In 1981 she received a Guggenheim Fellowship as well as a Medal of Excellence from Columbia University, and was appointed to the New York State Council for the Arts. Among her many plays, collections of poetry, and novels are *Natural Disasters and Other Festive Occasions* (1977), *Nappy Edges* (1978), *Sassafrass, Cypress & Indigo* (1982), the autobiographical *Betsey Brown* (1985), and *A Daughter's Geography* (1991).

MELVIN B. TOLSON (1898–1966). Although four years Langston Hughes's senior, Melvin Tolson is not technically considered a Harlem Renaissance poet. His first published collection of poetry, *Rendezvous with America,* appeared in 1944. He is best known, however, for *Harlem Gallery, Book I, The Curator* (1965), which won Tolson the American Academy of Arts and Letters annual award for poetry and playwriting. That same year, he won an endowed professorship at Tuskegee Institute. Unfortunately, Melvin Tolson died one year later of cancer.

MARGARET WALKER (1915–). Margaret Walker wrote *For My People* when she was only twenty-seven years old. She is known for the novel *Jubilee,* which, after thirty-four years of research, was published in 1966. Walker has been the recipient of many awards and honors, including the Yale University Younger Poets Award in 1943—making her the first African American to win such an honor—and a Houghton Mifflin Literary Fellowship in 1966.

BOOKER T. WASHINGTON (1856–1915). Educator, reformer, scholar, author, political leader, and activist, Booker T. Washington was one of the most influential African-American leaders of the early twentieth century. Reared in West Virginia, Washington worked in salt furnaces and coal mines as a boy. At the age of sixteen, he entered Hampton Institute in Virginia, where he worked part-time as a janitor to pay for his college expenses. Following further studies at Wayland Seminary in Washington, D.C., Washington returned to Hampton, where he joined its faculty. In 1881 he established Tuskegee Institute, a fledgling college that would become one of the foremost educational institutions for African Americans.

By the beginning of the twentieth century, Washington had received honorary degrees from both Harvard and Dartmouth. He had also dined at the White House, becoming the first African American to do so. His distinguished career included the publication of several books. *Tuskegee and Its People* (1905), *The Life of Frederick Douglass* (1907), and his autobiography, entitled *Up from Slavery* (1901), are some of his better-known works.

Richard Wright (1908–1960). Poet, novelist, essayist, journalist, playwright, communist, agnostic, and existentialist, Richard Wright is one of the most important writers of the twentieth century. Born into the impoverished, rural environment of Natchez, Mississippi, on September 4, 1908, Wright worked a number of hard jobs before arriving in Chicago in 1927, where he became deeply interested in communism. After moving to New York in 1937, Wright became Harlem editor of the communist *Daily Worker* and, later, vice president of the League for American Writers. His first book, *Uncle Tom's Children,* was published in 1938. But Wright may be most famous for *Native Son,* which was published in 1940. Some of his other well-known works include the novella *The Man Who Lived Underground* (1942), the autobiographical *Black Boy* (1944), *The Outsider* (1953), and *White Man, Listen!* (1995), which was published posthumously.

—— Books for Further Reading

ANTHOLOGIES AND COLLECTIONS

This is a list of anthologies and poetry collections that feature the works of many of the poets encountered in *Shimmy Shimmy Shimmy Like My Sister Kate*. Individual works by the authors are cited in the main text and the biography section of this book. An asterisk indicates that the book was written especially for young readers.

*Adoff, Arnold, ed. *I Am the Darker Brother: An Anthology of Modern Poems by Negro Americans*. New York: Macmillian, 1970.

*———. *The Poetry of Black America: Anthology of the Twentieth Century*. With an introduction by Gwendolyn Brooks. New York: HarperCollins, 1973.

Andrews, William L. *Classic Fiction of the Harlem Renaissance*. New York: Oxford University Press, 1994.

*Bontemps, Arna W., and Langston Hughes. *Popo & Fifina*. New York: Oxford University Press, 1993.

Chapman, Abraham, ed. *Black Voices: An Anthology of Afro-American Literature*. New York: Penguin, 1968.

———, ed. *New Black Voices: An Anthology of Contemporary Afro-American Literature*. New York: Penguin, 1972.

Early, Gerald, ed. *My Soul's High Song: The Collected Writings of Countee Cullen*. New York: Anchor Books, 1991.

Huggins, Nathan Irvin. *Voices from the Harlem Renaissance*. New York: Oxford University Press, 1976.

Hughes, Langston, ed. *Selected Poems*. 1959. Reprint, New York: Vintage, 1974.

———, ed. *The Langston Hughes Reader*. New York: George Braziller, 1958.

Johnson, James Weldon, ed. *The Book of American Negro Poetry*. 1922, 1931. Reprint, New York: Harcourt Brace, 1969.

Lewis, David L., ed. *The Portable Harlem Renaissance Reader*. New York: Viking, 1994.

———, ed. *W. E. B. Du Bois: A Reader*. New York: Henry Holt, 1995.

Miller, E. Ethelbert. *In Search of Color Everywhere: A Collection of African-American Poetry*. New York: Stewart, Tabori & Chang, 1994.

Randall, Dudley, ed. *The Black Poets*. New York: Bantam Books, 1971.

HISTORICAL STUDIES
AND OTHER RELATED BOOKS

The following are biographies and other historical studies of the Harlem Renaissance. For a more complete annotated listing of works about Harlem Renaissance writers, as well as scholarly books about the period and its people, see Ann Douglas's readable and informed bibliographical essay in *Terrible Honesty: Mongrel Manhattan in the 1920s* (New York: Farrar, Straus & Giroux, 1994). An asterisk indicates that the book was written especially for young readers.

Anderson, Jervis. *This Was Harlem: A Cultural Portrait, 1900–1950*. New York: Farrar, Straus & Giroux, 1982.

*Bernotas, Bob. *Amiri Baraka (LeRoi Jones)*. New York: Chelsea House Publishers, 1991.

Bontemps, Arna, ed. *The Harlem Renaissance Remembered*. New York: Dodd, Mead, 1972.

Harlan, Louis R. *Booker T. Washington: The Making of a Black Leader, 1856–1901*. New York: Oxford University Press, 1972.

Harris, Trudier, ed. *Dictionary of Literary Biography Series, Vol. 51. Afro-American Writers from the Harlem Renaissance to 1940*. New York: Gale Publishers, 1986.

Honey, Maureen, ed. *Shadowed Dreams: Women's Poetry of the Harlem Renaissance*. New Brunswick: Rutgers University Press, 1989.

Huggins, Nathan Irvin. *Harlem Renaissance*. New York: Oxford University Press, 1971.

Hull, Gloria T. *Color, Sex & Poetry: Three Women Writers of the Harlem Renaissance*. Bloomington: Indiana University Press, 1987.

Jacques-Garvey, Amy, ed. *Philosophy and Opinions of Marcus Garvey.* 1925. Reprint, New York: Atheneum, 1992.

Kellner, Bruce, ed. *The Harlem Renaissance: A Historical Dictionary of the Era.* New York: Methuen, 1984.

*Lawler, Mary. *Marcus Garvey.* New York: Chelsea House Publishers, 1988.

Lewis, David L. *W. E. B. Du Bois: Biography of a Race, 1868–1919,* New York: Henry Holt, 1993.

———. *When Harlem Was in Vogue.* New York: Oxford University Press, 1989.

*Lyons, Mary E. *Sorrow's Kitchen: The Life and Folklore of Zora Neale Hurston.* New York: Macmillan, 1993.

McKay, Claude. *Harlem: Negro Metropolis.* 1940. Reprint, New York: Harcourt Brace, 1968.

———. *Home to Harlem.* 1928. Reprint, Boston: Northeastern University Press, 1987.

Nichols, Charles H., ed. *Arna Bontemps–Langston Hughes: Letters, 1925–1967.* New York: Paragon House, 1990.

Rampersad, Arnold. *The Life of Langston Hughes,* Vol. I, *1902–1941: I, Too, Sing America.* New York: Oxford University Press, 1986.

*Rummel, Jack. *Langston Hughes.* New York: Chelsea House Publishers, 1989.

Wintz, Cary D. *Black Culture and the Harlem Renaissance Remembered.* Houston: Rice University Press, 1988.

*Witcover, Paul. *Zora Neale Hurston.* New York: Chelsea House Publishers, 1991.

～ GENERAL INDEX

‒ Index of First Lines

➶ About the Author

For years, Nikki Giovanni has been thinking, writing, and teaching about the Harlem Renaissance. Inspired by questions from a ninth-grade class, she gathered together a selection of poems by twenty-three African-American poets, and then added her own informed, and often poetic, commentary to create *Shimmy Shimmy Shimmy Like My Sister Kate.*

Nikki Giovanni is a professor of English at Virginia Polytechnic Institute in Blacksburg, Virginia. Her books for Henry Holt include *Grand Mothers: Poems, Reminiscences, and Stories About the Keepers of Our Traditions, The Genie in the Jar* (with illustrations by Chris Raschka), and most recently, *The Sun Is So Quiet* (illustrated by Ashley Bryan). She lives in Christiansburg, Virginia.